ADVANCE PRAISE

"This book shines a light on what should be a priority workplace issue – Menopause. The chapter on work provides valuable insight that will give many women the confidence to start a conversation in their organization about the support that could help with their symptoms and transform their working life."
Rachel Suff, Senior Policy Adviser, Chartered Institute of Personnel and Development (CIPD)

"Blending facts and statistics about Menopause with practical tips for dealing with symptoms, Kate Usher covers many topics relevant to Menopausal woman in today's society and encourages a gentle and curious approach to self-care."
Sarah Scarratt, Coach and trainer, NLP and Clean Language

"Many women are now working through Menopause; this book concisely explains their legal rights and the obligations of their employers to support them, as well as providing a valuable resource and advice on all aspects of life and Menopause."
Gemma Dale, Co-founder, The Work Consultancy

D0916511

"*Your Second Phase* is an important book for our times, and puts a complete discussion around Menopause firmly on the agenda. It is practical and informative at the same time as being supportive, gentle, encouraging and empathetic. Kate's writing style is engaging, witty, honest and raw, and she successfully lifts a lid on the challenges so many women want acknowledging and the questions they want answering. Nothing is off limits – relationships, esteem, dating, body and brain changes and how to give yourself permission to evolve and navigate the often rocky seas of Menopause. I highly recommend it and wish it had been available when I started my Menopause journey ten years ago – for my whole family to read."

Gill McKay, Coach, speaker and author,
Stuck: Brain smart insights for coaches

"For many women, the reality of Menopause and its impact is likely to come as a shock. It certainly did for me when I started my Menopause journey with Kate – a font of knowledge on the subject. This book is an essential read for anyone wanting to take control of their Menopause, or for those who are wondering whether they may be going through it. Some of us are lucky enough to escape with minimal symptoms but, for most of us, the impact of Menopause is significant. Far from being a medical textbook, this book is a light-hearted, easy-to-understand guide with plenty of anecdotes and exercises to help you make sense of the subject and your own personal experience. You will learn more about yourself,

your relationships and, most importantly, how to take care of both as you travail Menopause. Whether you are already experiencing Menopause, want to prepare for what's ahead, or if you are supporting someone else, Kate's humorous observations of our human experiences make this often awkward and 'secret' subject more accessible for everyone."
Natasha Wallace, Author, *The Conscious Effect: 50 lessons for better organizational wellbeing*

"Kate has created a valuable, comprehensive, go-to guide to help you coach yourself through all aspects of Menopause and beyond."
Diane Danzebrink, Therapist and Menopause expert and Founder, Menopause Support and #MakeMenopauseMatter campaign

"Kate's work here is a gift to understand more about the complex area of Menopause. We finally have a book that enlightens and taboo-busts, so we can all help the women in our lives to their second phase."
Perry Timms, MCIPD & FRSA, Chief Energy Officer, PTHR, and HR Most Influential Thinkers 2017-2019

Published by
LID Publishing Limited
The Record Hall, Studio 304,
16-16a Baldwins Gardens,
London EC1N 7RJ, UK

info@lidpublishing.com
www.lidpublishing.com

A member of:

businesspublishersroundtable.com

All rights reserved. Without limiting the rights under copyright reserved, no part of this publication may be reproduced, stored or introduced into a retrieval system, or transmitted, in any form or by any means (electronic, mechanical, photocopying, recording or otherwise) without the prior written permission of both the copyright owners and the publisher of this book.

© Kate Usher, 2020
© LID Publishing Limited, 2020

Printed by Gutenberg Press, Malta
ISBN: 978-1-912555-62-8

Cover and page design: Matthew Renaudin

Kate Usher

YOUR SECOND PHASE

Reclaiming work and
relationships during and
after Menopause

MADRID | MEXICO CITY | LONDON
NEW YORK | BUENOS AIRES
BOGOTA | SHANGHAI | NEW DELHI

CONTENTS

ACKNOWLEDGMENTS

There are many who have inspired me to write this book and many more who have helped me. There are many, too, who have shared their stories or sought my help. Massive appreciation to you all.

I'd like to thank, in particular, those who helped me with drafts, ideas, facts and other specialist input – Kathy Abernethy, Jan Adams, Ella Aziz, Kirsty Birnstiel, Carole Bozkurt, Dr Sue Brook, Julie Brown, Catherine Daley, Gemma Dale, Diane Danzebrink, Ruth Devlin, Hazel Dyason, Mel Haines, Jayne Harrison, Pauline Hill, Beth Hughes, Dr Alyson Jones, Jane Lewis, Parmjeet Mand, Gill McKay, Kate Mitchell, Gethin Nadin, Polly Plunkett-Checkemian, Perry Timms, Juliette Sacher, Sarah Scarratt, Suzi Sharples, Rachel Suff, Penny Tompkins, Karen Trewin, Maria Van der Veer and Natasha Wallace.

Jill Gatcum, thank you for your friendship. You have been an inspiration, a guide and the best friend a woman could ask for.

To the whole team at LID Business Media – your support and encouragement have been fantastic throughout.

To my amazing husband Neil and our fabulous girls Ava and Mae – you are the light in my day.

This book is dedicated to my adored brother Alasdair 'Bunny' who probably never thought I'd write a book but always believed I could.

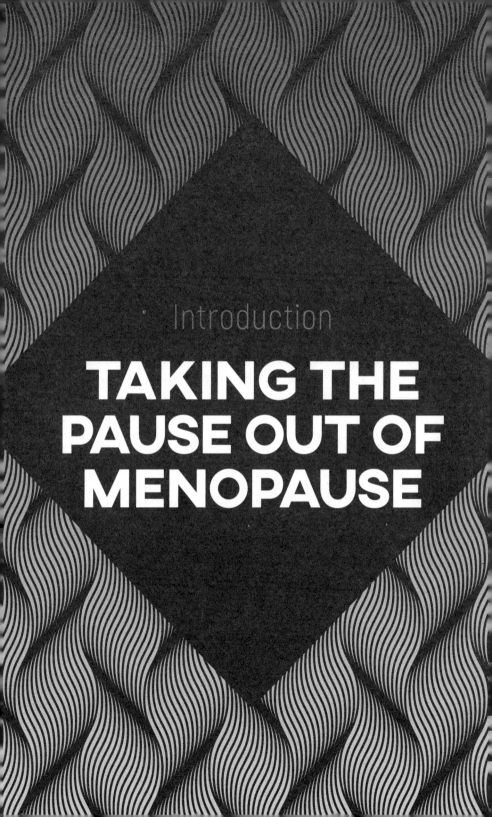

Introduction

TAKING THE PAUSE OUT OF MENOPAUSE

Great relationships are at the heart of every success story.

In an increasingly connected world, our ability to create, develop and maintain relationships has never been more critical. Our reliance on those connections we find and nurture is often unconscious. We are only aware of their importance when they are challenged.

Vital to building relationships, we identify and manage the small inflections and nuances in people's tone of voice, body language and written word, and respond appropriately. They are innate skills important to our success in our chosen careers and personal lives, developed as we have grown. We've watched, listened and considered. We've learned from our mistakes and moved on.

At the point we feel we're really on our game, Menopause arrives unannounced. For many, untold chaos ensues.

What was once easy is now complex, dogged by mood swings, bringing tears or rage with no warning or reason. Your confidence can be crushed by anxiety, depression and memory loss. You may struggle with the discomfort and social embarrassment of hot flushes or flooding (extremely heavy and unpredictable periods). You may gain weight uncontrollably. When you try and gather yourself to deal with some or all of it, you can be crushed by intense fatigue where even the most basic of activities requires a seemingly impossible effort.

Where you once intuitively responded to situations, comments or interactions, you now consider double-checking what you might say for fear of responding in a manner considered out of character. You no longer trust your judgment – at least not all the time. This wariness becomes infectious, as those around you tread increasingly gently in fear of a negative response. For some, Menopause instead creates a behavioural blind spot, where they are unaware of their unreasonableness until long after it has passed. There follows guilt and or remorse, both of which add insult to injury. It is a vicious cycle, which only acts to reinforce the downward confidence spiral, damaging relationships in a 360° sweep.

All of this happens at a time when you might be thinking of pushing on to the next level in your career, your ambitions firmly focused on a seat at the management or executive table or possibly changing careers altogether. Maybe your entrepreneurial spirit has just started to rev up, and there is no longer room for downtime. Perhaps your significant relationship is under pressure or in need of attention. Maybe you are single and want to find that special someone, and the management of your symptoms is not something you or they had bargained on. We live complex lives and your Menopause couldn't have come at a worse time.

There is never a good time.

When my peri-Menopause started in my 40s, most people I spoke to couldn't believe that a woman my age was experiencing it. There was virtually no information available and

I heard almost no one discussing it openly. There were, of course, a few lifelines in the form of programmes such as BBC Radio 4's *Woman's Hour*. If you were lucky, your Mum might talk about it (mine did not), or you had an older friend who shared her experience. I did, and I am forever grateful to her. She kept me sane and answered every question I had – multiple times. She also gave me something else that changed the path of my Menopause.

In my darkest hour, when I felt broken beyond repair, she took control and did the only thing she could – she used her knowledge, compassion and friendship to take me to the pharmacy and fill a basket with vitamins. For me, the contents of the wire crate were not the solution; it was the epiphany that while I couldn't control my symptoms, I could control how I responded to them and what actions I took next. This act of friendship and love began the process of piecing me back together again. A close personal relationship had revealed what was possible. It was where I first realized that relationships are critical to managing our way through Menopause – and how vulnerable they are during the very time we need them most.

During the depths of my own personal chaos I occasionally stumbled across articles and reports declaring that we could better manage Menopause if we just ate better (more fish, soya, or a rainbow of vegetables), exercised more (three times a week) or slept properly (eight blissful hours a night), and we would have our symptoms happily under control. It was all down to us. Social empathy appeared absent. I would have grown gills if I had eaten any more fish. I had ready access to a freezer full of edamame beans, a fridge full of soya yogurt and a harvest worth of vegetables. I drew the line at kale and quinoa, of course – who wouldn't?

Naturally, a balanced diet, regular exercise and good sleep are important regardless, before, during and after Menopause. It probably shouldn't even need saying, yet still does. However, the nature and severity of, and variation in, your symptoms is a genetic lottery, or down to the surgeon's knife. Period. Or rather, no period.

Having suffered extensively with my Menopause, I set out to study it and find out what was really going on, from societal perceptions to the gritty reality. So absorbed did I become – and so frustrated that it was not a subject that many were even prepared to talk about – that I made it my mission to do what I could to change all of this and help give women a sense of purpose during this time of their lives. I take the view that Menopause shouldn't be a pause, a time in which the best women can do is stumble through, stiff upper lip and no grumbles, hoping that this thing they don't understand and can't talk about will go away. They shouldn't have to put their life on hold and watch their relationships deteriorate and vanish in the process.

Much of the published material available on Menopause, an extremely valid and valuable contribution, is written by those in and around the medical profession. While there are symptoms affecting our physical and mental health to discover and understand, Menopause is also fundamentally a social issue.

I'm not a doctor or medical practitioner and, therefore, I have avoided too extensive and detailed a review of this aspect, instead focusing on us as human beings surrounded by human beings, the product of three million years evolving as social creatures. I'm not a lawyer either. Being a United Kingdom resident, this book references (mainly) the law of England and Wales as it stands at the time of going to press. Should this not be applicable to where you live, it will be important to seek specific assistance, especially for employment law, in your country or state.

After many years of coaching and talking with women, initially about work and relationships and later because of my own experience with work, Menopause and relationships, this book is written from the perspectives of active research, listening to women and personal reflection. It is the result of this enquiry, belief and commitment.

This book had many working titles as it unfolded, some obscure and some comedic. I have loved all of them for different reasons. It's played havoc with my filing system. It has the title it does today because I consistently talk about Menopause being the transitionary phase between the first and the second phase of your womanhood, that began at puberty. It's not the 'second half' of your life because we don't have a crystal ball – at least one that works. It's not a 'second life' because that has all sorts of connotations we don't want to get into. You may have noticed already, but I have capitalized the word Menopause throughout this book. While it is not technically correct, I believe that its impact warrants it.

The core message of this book is that your relationships – with yourself, with work colleagues, your personal relationships and those that don't yet exist – are not only vital to managing your Menopause, but can also thrive at this time and prepare you for your second phase of womanhood. They are the key; they create the infrastructure upon which we build our lives. During Menopause they are a safety net protecting us through extremes, providing comfort, sanity, reflection and advice. Their absence creates a level of isolation that compounds every complexity of Menopause.

The book, in turn, identifies your experience, skills, motivation, resilience and resources – together, they are what I term the 'superpowers' – you'll need to draw on to identify, maintain and develop your relationships when the wrecking ball begins to swing in your direction. They have already supported you through the first phase of your womanhood, however conscious of this you have been. Some may be dormant waiting for the call, others may seem to have deserted you. Be assured they're here for the second phase.

This book recognizes that Menopause can be complicated, emotionally and physically debilitating, yet at the same time provides an opportunity to drive a level of change that is only offered to women at this stage in life. Your second phase is open to being defined by you. The pause is over. Let's get on with it. Together.

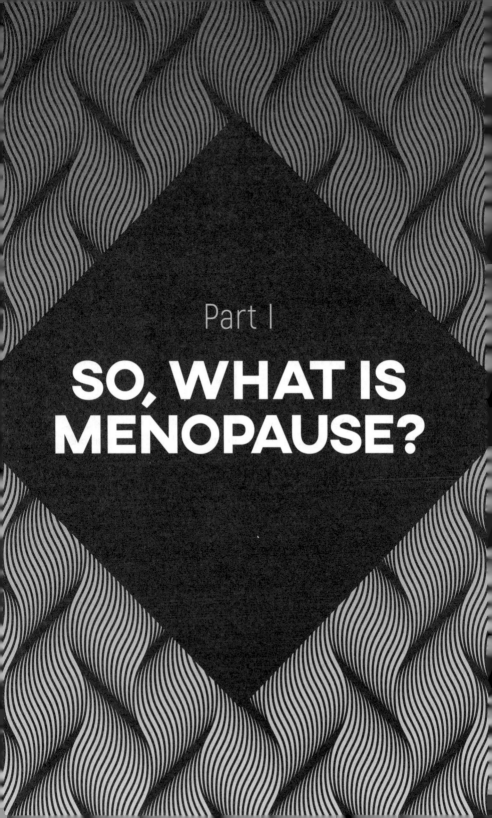

Part I

SO, WHAT IS MENOPAUSE?

Before we look at how Menopause affects our relationships, we need to know more about what it involves. While I am not medically trained, this information is readily available in the public domain. If, at this stage, like many women you know little about Menopause, this will be a useful grounding to take through the rest of this book. It will also help you gain some perspective when preparing yourself for discussions with those you interact with.

CHAPTER 1
MENOPAUSE FACTS AND FIGURES

As a society, we tend to view Menopause in its generality. We see it as an older woman's condition, a bit sweaty, a bit overweight but something not too bad, more of an inconvenience that women can manage on their own in the shadows. After all, isn't that what cardigans are for? For older women who need to take them off discreetly when they get hot? I can see why we think that. After all, those have been the only images we have seen in the media until now, but Menopause is so much more complex than that. It doesn't fit a social stereotype; it doesn't conform to specified limits or rules.

Your Menopause is as unique as your fingerprint.

Medically, Menopause can only be identified in retrospect. It is when you have not had a period for 12 months, effectively 12 months and one day. If you are one day short, sorry, but you start the countdown again from the beginning. It heralds the end of your reproductive years, signalling the end of your egg reserves. For some this will be a relief, while for others it will cause deep sadness and grief. It is important to note that should you have a bleed once you become post-Menopausal, you should seek medical advice

The average age of Menopause in the UK and the US is 51,[1] with the core period to experience symptoms being 45 to 55. However, one in every 100 women[2] in the UK experience Menopause before the age of 40. As a society, we assume that Menopause is an older woman's issue, but this is not the case. While rare, young women in their teens, 20s and 30s can have what is medically known as Premature Ovarian Insufficiency (POI). Experiencing Menopause at this young age is extremely difficult for a multitude of reasons, including society's visual and narrative presuppositions regarding age.

For those women who have a medically induced Menopause, which can be through cancer treatment or the removal of their ovaries (oophorectomy), this can of course occur at any age and is especially severe, as there is no gentle preamble. Psychologically in these instances, women need to deal with the medical condition that brought them to this point, plus an instant and extreme Menopause.

No woman lives in isolation; therefore, those around her will no doubt be exposed to her Menopausal symptoms as well. This is by no means a criticism; it is a recognition of the far-reaching impact of symptoms on all aspects of women's lives and the lives of those within their social networks.

There are many things about Menopause that make it a tricky subject to discuss openly, for women and those they interact with. It is still a social taboo, partly due to its wide-ranging impact on women's physical and emotional states. Another is the lack of objective and defined uniformity experienced from one woman to the next. In this respect, there are three key areas of variance.

CHAPTER 2
DURATION

What we commonly call Menopause is often the period during which we experience symptoms. On average, this can last for four to eight years,[3] but it's not uncommon for women to experience symptoms for longer. Menopause has three recognized phases:

1. Peri-Menopause – the time leading up to Menopause, when your hormone levels start to fall
2. Menopause – 12 months since your last period
3. Post-Menopause – your life after Menopause

A very small percentage of women continue to experience some symptoms for the remainder of their lives. While this is rare, it is no consolation if you are suffering from hot flushes, night sweats or vaginal atrophy decades after becoming post-Menopausal.

CHAPTER 3

SYMPTOMS

[PART ONE]

There are a wide range of symptoms, which can affect women psychologically, physically and emotionally. You may experience many or none. If you do experience symptoms, they can change as you move through your Menopause. Equally, you may sail through peri-Menopause without a single symptom other than unpredictable periods and find that your early post-Menopausal years cause you the most problems, or vice versa. Of course, your symptoms could continue throughout.

So, who gets symptoms and who doesn't?

On average, 75%[4] of women experience symptoms, 50% of which find that those symptoms can at times be detrimental to their wellbeing; 25% of women have severe symptoms that are extremely detrimental to their wellbeing, affecting their ability to function as they used to on a day-to-day basis. The lucky remaining 25% have no symptoms at all. We would all like to be in the last tranche, but sadly, it's a lottery. If you and three girlfriends sat around a table chatting and drinking tea, one of you would be wondering what the fuss was about, two of you would be finding your symptoms troublesome and one of you would be having a very hard time indeed. Lastly, the three of you experiencing symptoms could all be suffering from completely different things.

There are many symptoms of Menopause, and some are more well known than others. Hot flushes, while common – currently estimated at 79%[5] – are not ubiquitous. They are often used as the yardstick for diagnosis or dismissal, which is unhelpful and isolates many women further. Conversely, depression and anxiety, while extremely common, are often wrongly considered as unrelated to Menopause and, therefore, not treated in the right context.

The table below is a list of Menopausal symptoms, some of which you will already know and others you may not have associated with it. I have split them into three sections in descending order of occurrence, i.e. the superstar symptoms we all know about and hear of in the press, followed by those that we are starting to hear more about. Lastly, I have included those symptoms we rarely hear about. In most instances, this is because we feel buttock-clenching embarrassment discussing them in public, while for others it's simply that we never thought they were Menopausal symptoms before now. Gladly, through awareness this discomfort is slowly diminishing.

Take a minute to read over the list and tick the ones you think or know you are experiencing. This is important, because you will come back to this in the next chapter when we will look at their severity and impact.

	Tick here
The superstars – the ones we expect	
Hot flushes	
Night sweats	
Mood swings – angry outbursts to floods of tears	
Weight gain	
Irregular periods	
The social climbers – the ones we are starting to hear more about	
Insomnia	
Fatigue	
Anxiety	
Depression	
Panic attacks	
Loss of confidence	
Difficulty concentrating	
Memory lapses	
Loss of verbal recall	
Migraines	
Dizziness	
Breast pain	
Flooding – extremely heavy and unpredictable periods	
Loss of sex drive	
Brittle nails	
Dry hair	
Dry skin	
Itchy skin –in extremes cases, can feel like insects crawling over the skin	

The Z listers – the ones we don't hear enough about ... yet can be catastrophic	
Vaginal dryness/atrophy	
Cold flushes	
Recurrent urinary tract infections [UTIs]	
Increased susceptibility to thrush and bacterial vaginosis [BV]	
Incontinence [stress and urge]	
Loss of muscle mass	
Allergies	
Hair loss	
Unwanted hair growth	
Joint pain	
Stiff joints	
Gum problems	
Digestive problems	
Changes in body odour	
Snoring	
Sleep apnoea	

Now that you have read and ticked your symptoms off the list, I am sure that some of you are horrified by some of the symptoms, hoping that you don't encounter them. I can't promise you won't, because your symptoms are likely to change and undulate in severity before you get to your final post-Menopausal state.

CHAPTER 4
SEVERITY

This leads us to the severity with which you experience symptoms. For some, and sadly I was one of them, Menopause can take you to a very dark place. For others, the symptoms are simply annoying. This can and does change as the hormone production from your ovaries (oestrogen and progesterone) ebbs and flows before finally giving up and leaving you with your new status quo.

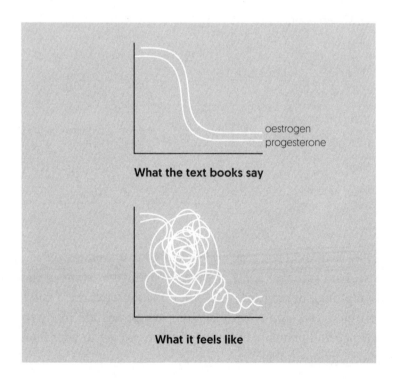

oestrogen
progesterone

What the text books say

What it feels like

I have been asked many times to describe what Menopause feels like for the unlucky 25%, often by those who will never experience it and those who are yet to. The best I have come up with to date is that it can be like having the worst flu, with a massive hangover, little sleep and intense morning-after anxiety, where you either burst into tears or struggle to contain pure vitriolic anger at anyone who even looks at you, all day, every day, for years. It can be a downward spiral which is hard to escape from. This sounds extreme and somewhat dramatic but, for some of us, that is how it is. It's not surprising that the Samaritans in the UK report that the highest rate of suicide among women was in the 50-to-54 age group in 2017[6] and the 45-to-49 age group in 2018.[7]

I would like to reassure you, though, that this – as with the other two variances (duration and symptoms) – is very much at the far end of a sliding scale. Every experience is valid and deserves empathy and support, not judgment.

CHAPTER 5
VARIATION, VARIATION, VARIATION

Each woman's Menopause is unique to them – one woman cannot be judged by another's experience. There is no standard solution nor a support package that can be appropriately applied.

The degree of variance, plus the nature of the actual outward and inward symptoms themselves, is one of the reasons that culturally many have been reluctant to openly discuss Menopause in work or social environments, causing it to be swept under the carpet as though it were in some way distasteful. This is, of course, a 'Catch 22'.[8] Women don't speak up because people find it an uncomfortable subject and find it easier to dismiss it than confront it. Unlike menstruation, which happens every month or pregnancy, which lasts nine months (if full term), Menopause has little uniformity and lasts for years. Yet, all of us have either known or interacted with a woman who was going through it, even before we ourselves started to be aware of our own Menopause. There is little else in life that has such a wide-ranging impact on all areas of life which, until recently, seemed to happen in secret.

We, as a society, have failed to communicate a simple message to women, advising what Menopause is, how it might impact us and the steps we could take, without swinging from the dismissal of 'typical mad woman' to horror stories of 'it's the end of the world and should be avoided at all costs'. We arrive at this phase of our lives uninformed and without the support structures needed. The lack of narrative and information that neither downplays nor scares us means that we have little in the way of commonly known signposts or conversation starters that we could call on at this time. If we had these, it would enable us to ask for help and support, with no stigma, shame or embarrassment from those we interact with, whether it be our colleagues or those we love.

It is entirely possible that we will spend a quarter of our career managing our Menopause, and a third of our life as a post-Menopausal woman. When you put it into perspective, it is no wonder that this generation of educated, informed and successful women want to bring this life event out of the shadows. In short, we are no longer prepared to take off our cardigans quietly and whisper in the shadows.

HORMONE REPLACEMENT THERAPY (HRT)

Before I begin, I need to state I am not a doctor and I cannot advise you whether to take HRT; therefore, my comments are simply my opinion. Some general observations are possible without medical training.

You will only be considering taking HRT if you are having a hard time with your symptoms, have a medically induced Menopause, have POI or, like me, have the early signs of osteoporosis (as well as a hard time). At this point you will need to consult your GP (General Practitioner) or a Menopause specialist[9] to discuss your options and the risks. If your GP doesn't feel comfortable prescribing HRT for whatever reasons, in the UK you can ask to be referred to one of the excellent NHS Menopause clinics or, alternatively, you could opt for a private clinic. If you are doing the latter, please ensure that they are a registered specialist recognized by a national body.

Opinions of HRT are divided into two camps. On one side there are those who say that it should be avoided at all costs due to the associated risks. On the other, they say that it is an essential part of women's health and that the benefits far outweigh the risks.

During my entire Menopause experience, at different times I have sat in both camps.

Few treatments for any condition are free of risks or side effects. HRT is a choice that every woman needs to make for herself. We should be provided with up-to-date information on risks and benefits to enable a balanced choice to be made. As with many treatments, the potential risks need to be weighed against the positive impact on the quality of life it will bring. HRT can be life-changing for many. The choice to take it should be commended, not belittled.

CHAPTER 6
SUMMARY

WHAT WE LEARNED

Your Menopause is as unique as your fingerprint. Every woman will experience their Menopause differently. In fact, one in four of us will experience no symptoms at all. For those of us who do, there is a long list of possible symptoms.

We may experience one or many, the degree of severity may be annoying or utterly debilitating, and we may experience them from anywhere between four to eight years – or perhaps even over a decade. This level of variance is what makes each woman's Menopause unique.

WHAT WE DID

You looked at the list of symptoms and identified those which you are currently experiencing or have experienced. Some may have come as a surprise, and with others you may have crossed your fingers, legs and everything else in the hope that they would never be part of your life.

We recognized that symptoms may come and go throughout Menopause due to our ever-declining hormone levels.

HOW THIS HELPS

Knowing that much of what we experience at this time of life is due to our declining hormones and not something more serious, such as a debilitating or life-threatening disease, means that we can take action and gain control for ourselves. The fear associated with not knowing robs us of control.

Knowing that you are on a journey enables you to prime yourself for the changes ahead.

Part II

YOU

You simply cannot experience successful and meaningful relationships with others without having an understanding and constructive relationship with yourself. The control you give yourself now and the vision you create for yourself beyond this point are reflected in all the other relationships you have now and in the future.

Therefore, it is important to consider you as you are now, and how you might be in the future.

CHAPTER 7

YOU, NOW

It is you experiencing Menopause and you transitioning to your post-Menopausal self. This is quite a journey and one that you cannot predict or define until you are in it. You cannot plan until you know. Therein lies a lot of the problem. Remember the horror and shock when your first period happened, blood in your knickers, oh no! You knew all along it was going to happen one day, and then it did. You may have had a lesson at school, your mum may have given you a book, you may have had a red-faced and whispered conversation with a friend or your sister, but nothing really prepared you for that moment. In many respects, Menopause is the same. Generally, your symptoms arrive when and how they arrive, and you have to face up to them.

Good news – this is where that face-off tips in your favour. This is the last hurrah for the hormones that have driven you along a continuous monthly rollercoaster since your first spotty outbreak, greasy hair let-down, tearful rant at your parents and yes, those bloody knickers.

In considering your relationship with yourself, I have split this chapter into two. First, you now – the present version, you 1.0 – and then future you, the version 2.0 you can create.

Not surprisingly, you can now look at the stuff that often concerns women in peri-Menopause and beyond. It's the state we don't often talk about because we don't connect symptoms to the rest of our experience. You are a whole person, so why wouldn't how you feel about and perceive your transitioning self be connected? This chapter is essentially about gaining perspective and giving you control, so that you can manage your experience. It's a critical first step. You can't hope to master relationships with others if you don't first master the relationship with yourself. That sounds like a tall order, a fiction, but it is not. You do have the power to do this.

First off, we look at your perceptions of yourself, how you judge yourself and the person you are becoming. We pick apart any critical self-talk that goes under the radar. Before you even draw breath to deny it, know that we all do it to some degree, it just depends on whether you can recognize it for what it is – a controlling and co-dependent partner or friend that lives in your head.

Next, we discuss the things that get all the airtime – symptoms – and how they affect this relationship. It would, of course, be ridiculous not to. You have ticked the list in the previous chapter, so you know what you are experiencing, but do you know what's really going on above the noise and general melee? This chapter looks at the interconnectedness of, and interplay between, symptoms, and how creating space around them enables you to identify which are causing you the most trouble, and which are the ring leaders. Teasing them apart in this way gives you the control needed to manage them.

This leads to the classification of symptoms by severity and impact. Not all symptoms that are severe have an impact on your quality of life, yet others, while not especially severe, can still have a major impact on multiple areas of your life. There are also those symptoms that are incredibly severe and have a massive impact. Recognizing these degrees gives you much-needed perspective.

The last section is the when, how and what of your symptoms. Put simply, when do they show up and are there any triggers you are inadvertently activating? Do your symptoms arrive with a fanfare or do they sneak up on you, cloaked in stealth? Recognizing their *modus operandi* is empowering, as is understanding your response. Do you react like any grown woman would and burst into tears and run out of the room, or do you metaphorically rip the head off the first unsuspecting person who dares to look at you? The chronology of your experience is supercharged; the power is in the information.

If someone had offered me the metaphorical bunch of carrots that this chapter represents instead of the stick I readily beat myself with when my peri-Menopause started, I would have grabbed it with both hands. It will take a bit of effort and thought, but it really is a carrot-or-stick choice that only you can make. For me it's got to be carrots, every time.

CHAPTER 8
YOU AND YOUR PERCEPTIONS OF YOUR TRANSITIONING SELF

Your relationship with yourself sits at the heart of your life experience. How you view yourself, what you tell yourself and what you consider yourself to be worth or able to do, the values you hold, silently drive your choices and behaviours. This is why we will start with you.

There is no point prettying up the outside if you feel like you can no longer identify with the woman on the inside.

As our hormones do a loop the loop before flying off into the sunset, many women report that they struggle to maintain the person they were before their peri-Menopause began, that their inner self has come under attack from their symptoms and their changing perceptions. Some struggle to hold on to her but one thing is for sure; many of us don't welcome the changes.

Our inner battle is reinforced subliminally by most images we see associated with Menopausal women. They are of women who are clearly 60-plus and are looking stressed, sweaty and waving a fan. Why do we not promote images of the many amazing, fabulous, dynamic women in their 50s and 60s alongside women in their 20s, 30s and 40s when we talk about Menopause? What are we afraid of? Realistically, the genie is out of the bottle. It is general knowledge that many women in active public life are of the average age to start experiencing Menopause. They don't stop looking fantastic, and they continue to be dynamic individuals. This really is no different for any of us. It's about time our perceptions were altered. This is important because we need to see and hear that women don't lose their essence or energy for life, both for themselves and society. It is part of recognizing our continued contribution and vibrancy in societal, professional and familial structures.

Conversely, I worked with one woman who lamented that she felt under pressure to age like a famous actress. She compared her figure, sense of style and general vivacity and believed that she was failing to keep up with this other woman's ability to defy the ageing process. In an ever-increasingly online, image-influenced world, there is a need to back off with the expectations of yourself. We all suffer from a bit of FOMO (fear of missing out) or 'not as good as' occasionally, but this is not the time to let it consume you. You are far better off seeking role models who make you feel good about yourself. We need to hear Menopause stories from all walks of life, as well as from our industry leaders, scientists, athletes and stars from the big and small screens. Those less exposed are usually balancing so many more pressures, existing on the edge of being overwhelmed. I have heard many inspirational stories from ordinary women, just like you and me. All this narrative is important; it gives perspective and support to each of us, while normalizing this phase of women's lives.

'THE CHANGE'

Our mothers called Menopause 'The Change' and for good reason. Your body is putting itself through incredible levels of change not experienced since puberty. Remember the anxiety, crippling self-consciousness, changes in your body shape, tears, tantrums, spots and body hair? Any of this sound familiar? The arrival of an intoxicating set of natural chemicals in our system – better known as hormones – shook us about a bit then, and hey presto they're doing the same thing as they make their exit. Trouble on the way in, trouble on the way out.

Yet we didn't call puberty 'the Change' and there wasn't any stigma attached. Everyone appreciated that it was natural, and in many ways prepared themselves for the unpredictability of those going through this change. As they changed, those around them adapted too.

Society has historically seen puberty as the point at which our adult self begins which, in our case, is womanhood. So too, unfortunately, has it regarded Menopause as the end of womanhood when, in reality, it is simply a transition to its second phase. As recently as the last century Menopause was referenced as a 'partial death,' rendering women deranged, deviant and unfeminine.[10] It is no wonder society ostracizes us and we fear it's arrival.

You have had many years to get to know the post-puberty you. You have developed a well-trodden path for your behaviours, how you manage problems and how you interact with others. You know your weaknesses and, very importantly, you know your strengths.

Your hormones have many jobs, not least to make you an arch placater, a negotiator, someone who can resolve conflicts, nurture others and put yourself at the back of the queue. These are the skills required for our evolutionary role as mothers and partners; even if you choose to be neither. Being supremely adaptable, we have put them to effective use both at work and play. The good thing is that once your hormones have receded to your new permanent state, you retain many of your skills. The other piece of positive news is that your ambitions, desires and needs have permanently elbowed their way to the front of the queue. You are once again focused on you.

FROM CRITIC, WITH LOVE

Many women report that there is definitely something different about them once they are post-Menopausal, not least that they worry less about what others think of them, and their inner critic is less judgmental. This is great news, as for many the transitional period is full of judgment.

Judgment comes in many forms: social, professional, familial or from yourself. We are born without judgment or prejudice; these are things we are given in the stories we were told as children and the rules that were either subliminally or directly passed to us. As we grew up, we rebelled, we reasoned away and we dismissed many of them, but others still lurk in the shadows, imperceptibly influencing how we feel about ourselves and other people.

They can be damaging and attritional, as they tend to be highly repetitive in nature, always occurring in association with specific behaviours, thoughts or feelings. Because of this, they instigate negative patterns that can feel and be extremely limiting.

The impact of your changing hormones on your behaviours and your emotional and psychological wellbeing can be considerable. If you are not your normal chirpy, calm or professional self, now is not the time to give yourself a good kicking. Your emotions may oscillate between the extremes of sadness and anger. Perhaps you feel so fatigued you can barely lift your head from the pillow; maybe your brain feels like it's treacle and your memory, well who knows where that's gone. Instead of disliking yourself for the new version of you, or drifting into the pit of despair, now is the time to show compassion and empathy to yourself. After all, this is not due to poor decisions or inappropriate actions – even if it were, you would still deserve support. This is something you have little control over.

You can always spot judgments by the modal verb used – as in 'should' or 'must':

- I/she/they should
- I/she/they must
- I/she/they have/has to
- I/she/they ought to

You do not start out saying these things to yourself. Yet, your self-talk is often full of them. It's part of being human. Therefore, it's more a case of either knowing them or recognizing them when they occur.

I am curious: when you hear yourself chastising yourself in this way, what would you like to have happen?

The key part of that question is 'like' – it calls for you to categorically say what you would like in the positive. If you find yourself saying what you don't want or what you want more of and less of, stop and reconsider. Gaining control is about moving into something positive, not focusing on the negative. Ask yourself again:

What would you like to have happen?

And then:

Is there anything else that your transitioning self needs?

Make a note of it, as it might surprise you. You don't want to forget it because it's the first step toward something better. Your journey has made its first tentative beginnings.

CHAPTER 9
SYMPTOMS
[PART TWO]

Let's start this process of considering your relationship with yourself with a deeper look at the things that get the most airtime: your symptoms. We introduced them in the previous chapter, and now we need to consider their impact.

Your symptoms are prima donnas, demanding and unpredictable. They can and do take women by surprise and rob them of their resources and their ability to manage in everyday environments. It's often the skills that women took for granted that are affected most rapidly.

Your Menopause is a journey and one that is full of ups and downs. It can feel all-consuming. However, some symptoms seem to be in the eye of the storm, while others are drawn into the swirling maelstrom surrounding it. If you are to gain any form of psychological upper hand, it's important to identify those that are troubling you the most at this specific time, and what happens when they do.

By separating them out, it enables you to isolate them from the pack and manage them one by one. It is too difficult to manage all your symptoms in one go without medical intervention. The symptoms themselves are depleting your ability to manage day-to-day life; therefore, taking on the whole pack is not a realistic expectation. Divide and conquer is the tactic here.

This section will feed directly into the other chapters of this book. Once you know which symptoms trouble you the most, you can seek assistance both in work and in your personal life. As people around you are likely to feel confused and uncomfortable discussing this topic, this will also help others to understand how to support you empathetically.

THERE'S A HERD IN THE ROOM

The cacophony from competing symptoms is intense; they can ride roughshod over your sensibilities and feel impenetrable. For some it can feel as though they are drowning or being trampled in a stampede – not just an elephant in the room, but an entire herd. Conversely, they have the stealth of a B-2 bomber, arriving at every important situation and interaction uninvited.

This is the point when you recognize and define how your symptoms are impacting your life. Those carefree halcyon days before peri-Menopause may seem a distant memory, when you knew the monthly rhythm of life, your strengths and your weaknesses. All that can seem to have disappeared and been replaced by something far less stable, with your symptoms jostling for supremacy.

If you are reading this to support someone else, yet you sailed through without so much as a problematic period, a warm brow or a sleepless night, thank your lucky stars and accept that not everyone is as lucky as you. Judging others by your own fortune is not helpful, whether that is in the workplace, socially or at home.

INTERCONNECTEDNESS

When Menopausal symptoms arrive, they can be so all-consuming that it is difficult to identify where one stops and another begins. They can entirely overwhelm you, which is debilitating when you are trying to maintain a career and private life.

Symptoms tend to hang out in packs, such that they influence each other. Because of this, it's important to be clear about those you have and how they connect to each other. I have frequently found that even those who declare a trouble-free Menopause have had a small cluster of symptoms. Maybe they have gained weight, lost their sex drive or suffered from anxiety, yet didn't attribute it to their Menopause. In most cases they have assigned it to age, genetics or lifestyle and, of course, all or any of these could be true. But when they are partnered with two or three other low-lying yet impactful symptoms, the Menopause flags are out and waving.

Let's take hot flushes, for instance, because they tend to crop up when you are under the slightest bit of pressure or stress, like when talking to your boss, meeting your child's new in-laws, or even meeting a prospective date. They can cause considerable anxiety, first because they occur when you want to appear cool and collected, not reduced to being sweaty and distracted, and second, because you can't predict when or where they might occur. Most women oscillate between the two. This anxiety can mean that you lose confidence socially, which can impact your ability to work, interact with colleagues or socialize with current or new partners, and can affect your desire or ability to be intimate.

The diagrams below show the potential groupings and inter-connectedness of symptoms and how they can negatively impact key parts of your life.

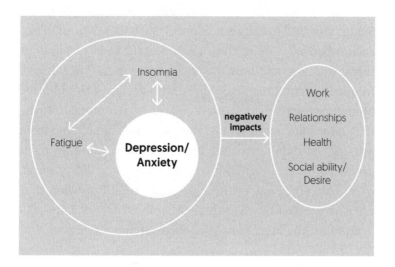

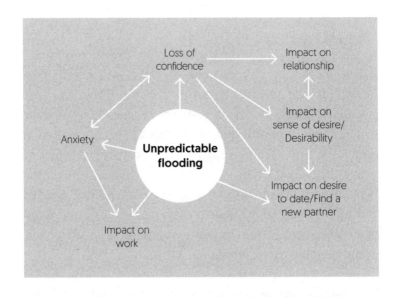

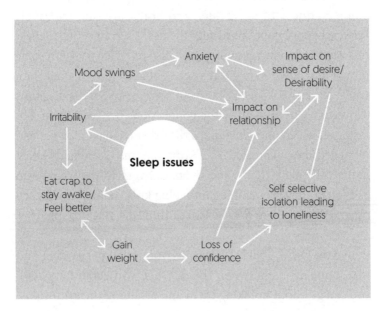

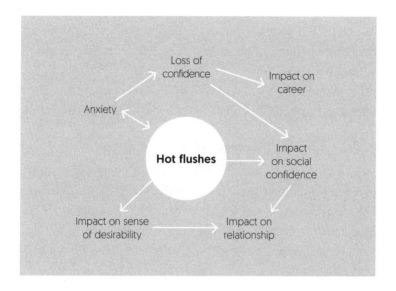

However your symptoms divulge themselves, connecting them in this way is not only revealing, but it also provides you with some insight into how you might reinstate some control. It would be a good idea at this stage to draw your own version of the diagrams above to begin to identify the connections between them. For instance, which ones encourage the others to have a bigger and more detrimental impact? Your symptoms may seem fairly linear in that x happens then y and so on. Conversely, they may seem as though they are jumbled into a big knot, bouncing off each other. Perhaps there may be two or three discrete groups.

Only you know which symptoms you are experiencing and the connections between them. Once you establish them, you can go about breaking them and disabling the symptoms.

As you look at your version of the diagrams above, can you see that there is one symptom that seems to sit at the centre of your experience? You tend to know if it is, as it affects all the other symptoms. If you removed it, the others would lose their intensity. You would feel able to regain that all-important control.

For example, let's say Susie is struggling with a sustained lack of sleep which leads to emotional outbursts and memory problems which, in turn, leads to anxiety. If Susie addresses her sleep issues, it will lessen or remove the intensity of her associated symptoms. It could reduce anxiety which, in turn, would enable improved sleep. We are deconstructing the network that Menopause has created, addressing its hold over you.

The critical piece here is knowing that you are seeking to manage just one symptom, not five or ten, and that once that one symptom is under control, you can eliminate those that depend on it. It is a much less daunting challenge.

This is a living exercise, as your core symptoms can and do change as you pass through the stages of your Menopause, before finally they fade to your post-Menopausal steady state. You'll have to keep track of the manner in which your network of symptoms reconstructs itself over time.

IMPACT

Having teased the knot of symptoms out into something far clearer and more understandable, it's time to be clear with yourself about their impact on your life. Impact is complex and is made up of three variables: frequency, intensity and scope.

Frequency and **intensity** are fairly self-explanatory, but their relationship can be complex. Intensity can be low, but the effect heightened by frequency. For example, joint pain can be at a low level, yet the fact that it never goes away can be highly attritional. Intensity can be high, but the effects mitigated by infrequency. For example, migraines can be utterly debilitating but might happen only once a month.

The breadth of areas of your life that are affected is the **scope**. This adds a further complication. For instance, vaginal dryness has a negative impact on your ability to have pleasurable penetrative sex, while severe vaginal dryness or vaginal atrophy can affect every area of your life, making it painful to sit or walk, and any suggestion of sex is literally that, a suggestion. I will discuss this further in Part 4: Personal.

Examples of symptoms with typically high frequency are hot flushes, night sweats, panic attacks, anxiety, memory loss, depression, bladder problems, vaginal dryness, vaginal atrophy, aching joints, fatigue and insomnia.

Those with typically high intensity are (and there is an overlap here with those of high frequency): hot flushes, night sweats, panic attacks, anxiety, depression, flooding, migraine, UTIs, thrush, bacterial vaginosis (BV) and vaginal atrophy.

Those with a wide scope are vaginal atrophy, hot flushes and night sweats, insomnia, anxiety and depression, panic attacks, fatigue and weight gain.

Please note, this is not an exhaustive list.

The process that follows is designed to provide perspective on your situation: to step outside of the day to day and look at each of your symptoms, in turn, objectively.

From your diagram in the previous section, fill in the table below with your five most troublesome symptoms.

This is a traffic light or RAG table. You will need to identify the impact of each of your symptoms by labelling them Red, Amber or Green – hence RAG – by frequency, intensity and scope. **Red equals high levels** of frequency, intensity and wide scope, **amber moderate** and **green low**.

The symptom labelled red is probably at the core of your experience and is the one that will have the greatest impact on your day-to-day life and equally the greatest impact if you manage it. Conversely, those symptoms with only amber or green rankings, while annoying, are probably not having a marked impact on your life. The symptoms labelled red carry the most impact and will return to you the greatest sense of control.

Just the process of gaining perspective and focus on what your symptoms are, how they connect to each other and

	Symptom	Frequency	Intensity	Scope
1.	...			
2.	...			
3.	...			
4.	...			
5.	...			

their impact gives a sense of control, especially if your symptoms seemed to be an indiscriminate mass of upset.

You now have two sets of information. Do they align – does the symptom with the highest impact sit at the centre of your symptoms driving the others? The likelihood is yes. Sometimes, however, there may be more than one; if so, move on to the next section with two or more symptoms as identified.

CHAPTER 10
THE WHEN, HOW AND WHAT OF IT

In this section we will be looking at the key symptom you have identified. If there are two or three, you can run through this as many times as needed. The purpose of this is to help you understand the landscape of your Menopause symptoms, to tease the cycle of event and response apart so that you gain a greater understanding and develop a strategy to deal with them.

WHEN

When does your symptom show up? Is it a night-time thing, day thing or is it indiscriminate? Is it when you are under any form of stress or can you state that if you eat x or do y then z will occur? Are there specific situations or environments that either cause more anxiety or frequency? What are your triggers, if any? It is important to note that triggers are not always apparent; sometimes there simply aren't any.

One woman I worked with had brain fog, loss of verbal recall and memory loss. She felt that it affected her most of the time but was definitely at its worst at work. She found this incredibly distressing, and it negatively impacted her ability to speak publicly, whether that was in a one-to-one or one-to-many situation. She felt that she simply couldn't guarantee that she'd know what to say or be able to remember the full sentence once she'd begun to speak. It made her feel useless, despondent and depressed. Without a doubt, it was affecting her career, personal relationships and social confidence. This type of fear-based isolation and withdrawal is not uncommon during Menopause. The British Menopause Society (BMS) reports that over a third of women feel less outgoing in social situations.[11]

If your symptom is utterly unpredictable then, by its very nature, it causes stress. Flooding is an example of this. The not knowing if and when it will happen can be extremely difficult for many women, as is the need to carry considerable amounts of sanitary ware plus clean underwear at all times. Many women have complete changes of clothes in their lockers at work just in case.

When does your key symptom show up – does it have a trigger or simply occur?

HOW AND WHAT

How does a particular symptom show up and what do you do when it does? What we are trying to establish here is the chronology of the event, from the first sign that things are happening to the last and our reactions throughout. Some women are not aware of their symptoms until after the event. Emotional outbursts – tears and anger – are prime examples of this. Women can believe their response to a situation is completely normal or appropriate until afterwards or when someone calls them out. This often causes considerable remorse, self-loathing or negative self-judgment.

For example, I never had any problems sleeping in my life. I had the gentle sleep of a baby until peri-Menopause, when it all ended. The rapid decline in progesterone meant that I struggled to get to sleep, but once I did, I was awakened repeatedly by night sweats and had to start the slow and painful process all over again.

I find the term 'sleep hygiene' somewhat unpleasant. There is almost an insinuation that you are unclean if you can't get to sleep. I also find it somewhat condescending, and quite frankly that isn't helpful at 2am. Having said this, however, when I went back through the period leading up to my night-time struggles, I found that there were a few things that I was doing that were not helping at all. Checking my phone before I went to bed was one of them. This was the death knell to a solid night's sleep, because of two key factors:

1. Blue light. As we all know this plays havoc with our circadian rhythms, telling our brains that it's day and not night. One simple peek to check the weather – my usual excuse – was enough to change my fragile rhythm to something akin to freestyle jazz, and that was then that, for the rest of the night.

2. Following my momentary weather check, I would often read through emails, texts and social media. I would then, in the wee small hours, ruminate over something, a problem, a solution, something somebody had or hadn't said. Whatever it was, my brain would get into the nuts and bolts of it just at the point I was hoping for a fluffy pillow to take me away.

Our decline in hormones is not something we can control without intervention; however, we can influence or control many of our own behaviours or responses. I have learned that I have to resist the lure of the phone if I want to sleep; if I don't, I know I have to pay the price of a very restless night and not being on my game the next day, at least until I've had a couple of strong coffees and so begins another behaviour that doesn't help sleep. But that's another story.

Below is my sleep, or lack of sleep, chronology.

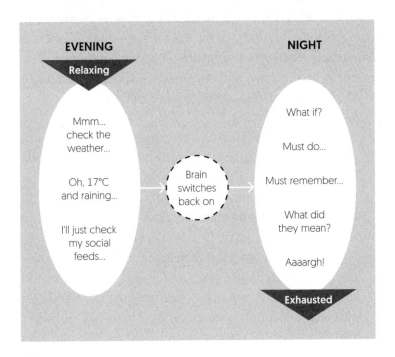

The point is to write the chronology of the event out in full. As tedious as this sounds, it often reveals steps you hadn't considered. You don't magically walk past the newsagents and end up with a bumper chocolate bar half eaten. You have to have gone in, selected it, bought it, unwrapped it and slipped it in your mouth before you get to that point, or at least that's how I do it.

I often find that it is most revealing if you write the symptom in the middle, with the aim to work forward to identify what happens once the symptom reveals itself, returning to the middle to work backwards toward your first awareness of it.

Working forward, ask yourself the following question:

"And when [symptom], then what happens?"

And then ask yourself:

"And then what happens?"

Ask the last question as many times as you need to run out of answers. This can go on for a while. Once this is done, go back to the middle and ask yourself:

"And when [symptom], what happens just before?

And what happens just before [previous answer]?"

Again, ask yourself this as many times as you need to, to get back to your first inklings, and even further if you have a sense of any triggers. What comes out can be very revealing.

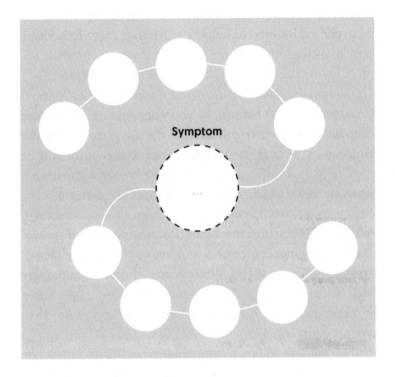

As you went through this process, did you have any moments of realization? Were there any times when you thought it was like x and it's really like y? With the process laid out in front of you, are there any signals that your symptom is on its way? Are there things you can do to mitigate or ease the symptom, or at the very least your stress response to it?

For example, are there some things that happen every time or most of the time? Are there any activities that you can do to lessen or mitigate them? Stopping myself from looking at my phone helped me to sleep. For symptoms such as flooding, where there aren't triggers, is there something you can do for yourself that lessens the impact? Obviously, carrying sanitary ware and clean underwear will lessen the stress levels at the time. I will talk about this in greater detail in Chapter 20.

If you look at what happens to you when you are in the thick of it, what are your reactions, how do you respond? Do you go to an extreme or do you withdraw, either internally or physically, to a different space? I spoke to one woman who, when she felt a hot flush coming on while she was in a social environment, would run from the room seeking sanctuary outside. She felt intense embarrassment over her sweaty and flushed appearance and couldn't cope with the idea of everyone staring at her. While many of us can empathize with her response, by running out of the room many times an evening, all it did was draw more attention to her than any hot flush could.

Again, are your perceptions of people's responses accurate, or are you thinking about this from your own perspective? Is everyone really looking at you, are they all actually judging you, or is that your own judgment of yourself? It is more than likely that they don't understand or know what is going on. Did you recognize Menopausal symptoms in other women before yours started? I know I didn't. They may have an inkling but don't want to raise the subject just in case they offend you.

It is very much time to reassess your judgments of yourself and the responses of others.

Is what you think is going on really what is happening? Do you metaphorically run from the room, simply sweat it out or somewhere in between?

Given the chronology of your symptom, list its triggers. Next, write what you can do differently to limit the activation of each trigger.

Trigger	What you can do differently to limit its activation
1. ...	...
2. ...	...
3. ...	...

Given that you may not be able to influence when or how your symptom occurs, you can control what happens next and how you respond. Given all of that, what can you do differently that will help what happens next?

What you can do differently to help what happens next
1. ...
2. ...
3. ...

Understanding the connectedness of symptoms and our response to them when they show up is like shining a searchlight on them. It's amazing what shows up. I have guided you to shine that light in certain places and will continue to do so as you proceed through this book.

Gaining control here will empower you to look ahead to the Future You with confidence. Every little thread of control you regain now builds to a point where suddenly you feel like you are back at the helm.

SELF-CARE

While this is a fashionable term for looking after yourself, I like its simplicity. It means what it says. During Menopause, things that you would normally have taken for granted as being part of your everyday routine go by the wayside – just at the point you need to be doing more of it. Menopausal symptoms, in general, don't inspire you to jump off the sofa and get moving. If anything, they do the exact opposite. Many women simply want to curl up with a drink and whatever comfort food they prefer.

This really is the point at which you have to put your health first. During and after Menopause, you are at greater risk than you were before of cardiovascular disease and osteoporosis. As we will discuss in Chapter 37, you are also more prone than ever before to weight gain, which puts you at risk of numerous cancers. All in all, there are enough reasons to take this seriously. While I appreciate that this is not a message many of us want to hear, there are some basic principles we should all adhere to – and each requires commitment:

Exercise more and get a sweat on. A casual stroll on the treadmill or around the park, while lovely and may help you clear your head, are not enough. You need to put some serious effort in. There are lots of things you can do. Try to incorporate load-bearing exercises (power walking, running, dancing) for your bones that will help with osteoporosis. We naturally lose muscle as we get older, so muscle-building exercises are highly beneficial. Combine these with some form of stretching for flexibility. Create an exercise plan and build it into your weekly routine – try and achieve three one-hour sessions a week.

Eat less and eat better. Should you have indulged or binged prior to Menopause, you can no longer do so. In fact, as your metabolism naturally slows with age, you will need to moderate your eating patterns. Incorporate more vegetables, fruit, nuts and pulses in your diet. Aim for a variety of colours and sources, and always seek balance. Again, some form of planning and routine is beneficial.

Cut down on alcohol. I know this may have scary implications for your social and leisure life, but alcohol is bad for you on so many levels. Cut it out if you can, cut it down if this is more practical or desirable. Have several consecutive nights a week that are alcohol-free. Replace alcoholic drinks with non-alcoholic alternatives. Drink no more than 14 units a week. To put this into context, a bottle of wine is approximately 10 units. Lastly, if you are drinking, try not to binge.

Stop smoking. We all know that smoking is terrible for your health. It is also highly addictive and, because of this, to stop you need to be resolute. There will be times when you will want nothing more than a cigarette, and you would crawl over broken glass to get one. Prepare yourself and get on with stopping. You really are worth it. Your GP will be able to help with this, whether it's with patches, gum or cessation classes. If you find that these are not available in your area, your local pharmacist will be able to help. I should add that vaping is not giving up. It is early in its existence and not enough is yet known about its health impact. When thinking about what you breathe, treat vaping as smoking. If you do smoke, stop.

These practices shouldn't be considered as stripping the fun out of your life. A mindset shift will be required if this is how it feels. If it persists, you will always be battling against a sense that you're being denied. Instead, think about the contribution it is making – what it's giving you. Exercising, eating healthily, drinking less and stopping smoking will make you feel more energized and will positively benefit your relationship with yourself and with others – and where you wish to find new relationships.

CHAPTER 11
FUTURE YOU

We are told by the media that women in their 50s feel invisible. Quite often the subtext to that is that our ambitions and desires evaporate as well. It's an interesting if ridiculous viewpoint. Many journalists and senior TV production roles are held by women 50+, hence why we are seeing more in the media about Menopause. Having turned 50, I have long white and platinum hair and am post-Menopausal – the heralded flags of ageing – and I can say with some confidence that I am not noticing any invisibility traits or loss of drive yet.

But many of us refuse to fit into an outdated stereotype of what a woman over the age of 50 should look like, and this rebellion opens the door to possibility. That desire to lead and not be led, to be yourself, to stick two fingers up at those who think they know it all, is not just for puberty, it's for Menopause as well. The second phase of your womanhood is calling you. It may not feel that way, but it is.

You know those signposts in quaint villages giving you directions to multiple destinations? You are effectively standing at a junction underneath one of those signposts deciding which way to go. Instead of Nether Wallop or Upper Snodbury, you are being asked to decide which way you will live your life, how you will go about it and with whom. These are big decisions, and ones that we usually pass to fate. Few consciously decide on a direction, which is unfortunate. If you don't decide, no one else will, and you could miss one of the greatest opportunities given to women. Who you will become and how you live your life is for you to define.

Once you have put a bit of space around your symptoms and stopped beating yourself up, it's time to think about the you that you are becoming. It's easy to believe that this transitionary phase will never end, but it will, and you will become a different version of yourself, no matter how subtle. Many women report that they are more confident, more focused and freer to pursue their interests. As with every ending in life, it is also a beginning and, as such, it brings opportunities.

Of course, if you were one of the many who had problematic periods or even endometriosis,[12] the mere suggestion that you could be released from the monthly tyranny of menstruation is something of a relief.

This section focuses directly on what might be and which direction you might choose. As such, you will refer back to it throughout this book. Your forthcoming ambitions for yourself will directly influence your career and personal relationships.

First, there is the important business of looking forward and not backwards. This might seem obvious and really it is, but in this youth-obsessed culture we find ourselves in, it is all too easy to slip into wishing we were 20 again. This is damaging and unrealistic. You have lived a life and so has your body; therefore – extreme plastic surgery withstanding – you cannot resemble your or anyone else's 20-year-old self. Give yourself a break! Before you can successfully achieve your future, you have to turn to toward it. Relish your past if you have happy memories but leave it where it belongs and move on.

Next, we will look at where you are now and where you might like to be in six core areas of your life: health, fitness, work, money, love and intimacy, and friends and family. This will enable you to identify what needs attention and where you most need to put your focus in order to achieve your ambitions.

Once you have identified the core areas of your life that need attention, we get to the exciting part: your five-year plan, focusing on where you might like to be, what you might like to be doing and with whom you might like to be doing it with. Most important of all, what and who will you be? You are the key driver here, as you are the one who is changing.

Your ten-year plan is a hope for what the future might hold, a further development of your five-year plan. I find that in my practice, women often feel that it is an opportunity to connect with a deeper sense of where and what they wish to be in the future. Often even more so than a five-year plan.

This section is about optimism, opportunity and ambition. There is a need to focus on the future, because it is coming up fast. Your choices matter; you could play it down or you could dream BIG. Go on, I dare you!

CHAPTER 12
WANT TO TURN BACK THE HANDS OF TIME?

At this point, I am always reminded of a woman I met at a party nearly ten years ago. She was in her mid-50s, had a great job, a new and fulfilling relationship and her children were grown up and successfully making their way in the world. From the outside she had it all, including a very flashy soft-top sports car. As we chatted later that evening, she revealed that even with all of this, she wasn't happy with her lot, as she felt that she was "not what she was" when she was in her 20s. I was stunned. I asked what made her think that, and she rolled off a list of reasons lamenting the changes in herself, both inside and out. She continuously compared herself to her 20-year-old self.

All this was accentuated by her daughters, who were in their 20s and brimming with youthful beauty and potential. She compared herself in every way, and wanted those years, that physique and that precious innocence back.

That conversation has never left me. As I hurtle toward my mid-50s, with young and beautiful daughters, I am in many ways more empathetic to her anxieties, yet a part of me wonders what choices she made as she transitioned to her post-Menopausal self.

If you have children or family members who are in their early 20s and full of potential, it is easy to look on longingly, wondering where the time has gone, wishing you could go back and do it all again. This is a unicorn moment; in fact, it's a sparkly unicorn moment – they are even harder to come by – it's one that can be extremely damaging as you can waste many years looking back instead of looking forward at what might be available to you, should you choose to live it. You are not 20, you will never be 20 again; in fact, you will never be the age you were five minutes ago, again. To expect it is both unrealistic and damaging to your self-esteem. Expecting yourself to be a mirror image of that young woman is not fair. You can't be her again and, to some degree, why would you want to be? Remember all the angst, naïvety, poor decisions and unsureness that came with that time of life? Take the rose-tinted spectacles off and remember that time of life in its entirety. Be kind to yourself.

And this leads me on to the rest. You can choose many things in life. If you choose to wallow in self-pity and 'what might have beens', then your post-Menopausal life looks bleak. On average, you will live over a third of your life as a post-Menopausal woman. Because of this, there is much at stake.

It is for you to define, to form into a life that makes you smile. Your past is your past and your future beckons.

As with everything, it's your choice!

CHAPTER 13
DREAM BIG

For you to maximize your life as a post-Menopausal woman and to make the most of new beginnings, you must pay attention to your ambitions both for yourself and your life. Doing this will give you a real-life superpower. It will enable you to focus on not only the future, but one that is curated by you, for you. It is super because it will act like a beacon even on the darkest of days.

During your Menopause, everything about you is calling for you to take stock of where you are in life today and where you might be tomorrow, and to lay down habits that will take you through into later years. You could, of course, choose to do nothing, to prevaricate, but we all know nothing good comes of that. Therefore, it's important to think about where you are now, and where you might like to be.

With this in mind, let's put a stake in the ground. Below is a blank scale representing six areas of life – health, fitness, work, money, love and intimacy, and friends and family.

Where would you mark yourself today, where **0 equals nothing going on** and **10 equals smashing it**? Rate it honestly; no one is watching.

This is not a competition, but an activity in self-reflection. If you look at the following scales and think that everything is going to hell in a handbag, that's OK because you can choose to do something about it. You are not alone in thinking this, I can assure you. Menopause can challenge your sense of self at every level. You are a human being who has a lot going on – take a deep breath.

Health

| 0 | 1 | 2 | 3 | 4 | 5 | 6 | 7 | 8 | 9 | 10 |

Fitness

| 0 | 1 | 2 | 3 | 4 | 5 | 6 | 7 | 8 | 9 | 10 |

Work

| 0 | 1 | 2 | 3 | 4 | 5 | 6 | 7 | 8 | 9 | 10 |

Money

| 0 | 1 | 2 | 3 | 4 | 5 | 6 | 7 | 8 | 9 | 10 |

Love & Intimacy

| 0 | 1 | 2 | 3 | 4 | 5 | 6 | 7 | 8 | 9 | 10 |

Friends & Family

| 0 | 1 | 2 | 3 | 4 | 5 | 6 | 7 | 8 | 9 | 10 |

The scales are like a walkway, a path; you can step onto them and imagine yourself walking up them. You could hopscotch them if you prefer. My suggestion is do it quickly, as overthinking it often skews the result.

Given you are where you are today, what would you like to have happen?

Take each of the areas in turn and think about where you are on the scale, what it is that you love about this part of your life, what's not so great and what needs your focus and attention. Even if you have scored a high number, there are always things that we want more of, or maybe a little less of x to enable you to have a little more of y.

Don't hold back or be apologetic, this is the time to stretch your ambitions. The end of the path needs to be attainable yet be more than you might previously have thought possible.

This is an opportunity to think of a time without your symptoms, without the mania that is Menopause. For those of us who are having a particularly hard time, we can no longer remember what life was like before all this began. This has its advantages, as you will definitely be different at the end of this process; for others, it's likely to be a little more subtle. With the change in your hormones, you will naturally and without conscious thought be focusing on yourself and the next phase of your womanhood.

I have lost count of the women who have told me that they have changed their lives since becoming post-Menopausal.

Some women change careers, while others follow an aspiration or notion long suppressed, and others start a new relationship. This phase of life is the clarion call for your ambitions.

While completing the chart, put another marker where you think you might like to be. One caveat is that not everything needs to be a 10. Sometimes being in the middle is just as it should be. This is not a compromise, but a choice.

Perhaps you are where you want to be; but if you are not, it could simply be that you haven't stopped to think about things in this way, or that you thought you were doing all right. But on reflection this is not the case, or possibly you knew you were nowhere near where you wanted to be and now that you see it in black and white, you know something has to change. Whichever you are, this is a time to think about where you are now and where you want to be, no matter how big or small the change might be.

CHAPTER 14
FIVE- AND TEN-YEAR PLANS

Five and ten years may be common in planning terms, but because of the time they represent, they can usefully take us up through the phases of Menopause and beyond, so we'll use them to create some structure.

A lot can change in five or ten years. You can turn your original thoughts on their head, you can embed them more deeply or tweak them here and there. It is important, however, to have an idea of what it is you would like to be doing, not least because at some point in the future you will retire from work and have a lot more time on your hands.

When focusing on the five-year plan, I have some questions for you. They are pretty simple, yet they will get you thinking about what life could be like in the future. This process will enable you to daydream, get out of the symptoms and the physicality, and to focus your mind on something positive and on something that makes you feel good. In addition to this, it signposts that you are on a journey, and one that you will have increasing levels of control over.

This exercise is quick and simple, yet highly effective. Many women find that the questions, while seeming too easy at first, continue to crop up for some time afterwards, forcing them to consider their answers at a much deeper level.

Each of the tables below begins with a big question. There follow some additional complementary questions to explore your thoughts a little further and to ground your answers. It helps you make the plan real. It's just as easy to dismiss a bullet point list as it is to create one, so we have to add depth and ground them in reality. All the questions are very much about you, so go around the loop as many times as you need to.

Vision	
For the next five years to go just the way I'd like, it will be like what?	… **A**
When it's like [**A**] is there anything else about [**A**]?	…
For it to be like that, I'll be like what?	…
What will I see/hear when it's like [**A**]?	…
How will I know it's like [**A**]?	…

Where	
In five years' time, where do I want to be?	… **B**
When I am [**B**] is there anything else about [**B**]?	…
For it to be like that, I'll be like what?	…
What will I see/hear when I am [**B**]?	…
How will I know I am [**B**]?	…

What		
In five years' time, what do I want to be doing?	...	C
When I am [C] is there anything else about [C]?	...	
For it to be like that, I'll be like what?	...	
What will I see/hear when I am [C]?	...	
How will I know I am [C]?	...	

Who with		
In five years' time, with whom do I want to be doing it with?	...	D
When I am with [D] is there anything else about [D]?	...	
For it to be like that, I'll be like what?	...	
What will I see/hear when I am with [D]?	...	
How will I know I am with [D]?	...	

If you have done this and have a sense of dissatisfaction, pay attention to it. Find where it resides, whether it be on the inside of your body or the outside. Once you have located it, does it have a size or a shape? What kind of dissatisfaction is it? Sit with it and see if anything comes up. Be curious; you may find that going through the questions again will bring up something new.

Have you ignored some kind of desire, through fear or judgment, have you dismissed something before it had a chance to be heard, or is it simply that it's not what you thought it would be? Is it enough or do you want more?

For this superpower to work, your five-year plan must entice you forward, it must glow with optimism and opportunity. If yours is full of mundanity, is this where you want to be in five years' time? Remember this is a future curated by you, for you.

NEXT STEPS

It would be remiss of me to move on without asking you to think about what you need to do to be living the life you have just defined in five years' time.

As with all things, small steps are the best way to achieve anything. First, because they are easy and can be done, and second, you can accumulate them quickly into bigger steps.

A good example of this was when I decided to start running. I was heavier than I had ever been, I had the beginnings of osteoporosis and generally needed to take considerable action. At the age of 50, I could not run for the bus. It was not my gift by any means. Once I had made the decision, it took me a few weeks to find the next step, which turned out to be an app on my phone, which took me from puffing and panting over a few yards to running 5K three times a week. I can assure you it was not a smooth path; my 50-year-old body was not ready for the change, I injured myself a couple of times, had to take time out, and start right back at the beginning again.

The important point for me was that my mind was resolute. I was going to do running. It was something for me and only me. It took nearly a year for it to become habitual. I am now compelled, but for a long time I had to schedule my runs in. I roped in my family to get their support and encouragement and celebrated each tiny milestone with them. I took numerous small steps – literally – which accumulated into achieving my goal.

If you want something for yourself in five years' time that is different from your life now, what small steps do you need to take to make it happen? If it is a stretch, I highly recommend breaking it down to even smaller steps. If I had tried to run even 1km at the beginning, I would probably have given up.

Given that small steps make big changes, what small steps can you take to get to your **A**, **B**, **C** and **D**?

	...
A	...
	...
	...
B	...
	...
	...
C	...
	...
	...
D	...
	...

Onto the ten-year plan.

While managing a period of such intense flux and change, you will need a plan for ten years based on what you have set out and achieved in your five-year plan. It is a cumulative exercise. The gap between five and ten years is considerable; both you and the world around you can be completely different.

There is only one key question here, plus the usual complementary questions similar to those you answered for your five-year plan. Just as before, all these questions are very much about you.

If circumstances change and you turn everything upside down, this is not failure. You may still want the same outcomes but need to take a different route to achieve them. You may decide that it's no longer applicable, and that your ideas have changed. Either way, the important thing to remember is that this is about you, and what you want for yourself. As your hormones ebb away, your ambitions will become far more important than they have been for a very long time.

Ten-year plan	
For my life to be just the way I'd like in ten years' time, it will be like what?	... **E**
When it's like [**E**] is there anything else about [**E**]?	...

For it to be like that, I'll be like what?	...
What will I see/hear when it's like [**E**]?	...
How will I know it's like [**E**]?	...
What will others see/ hear when it's like [**E**]	
What support or resources will I need?	

Having a five and ten-year plan will not only enable you to focus on moving forward, it will give you some much-needed perspective when your symptoms are turning everything upside down. It will shed some light when things feel pretty dark. They are devices to hold onto, sources of stability and perspective.

If journaling is your thing – and it's not for all of us – keep a journal on how you are progressing toward your plans.

CHAPTER 15
SUMMARY

This chapter is split into two key sections: **You Now** and **Future You**. The most important person is you and your relationship *with yourself*. You are the one experiencing this change, and you are the one who is having your view of the person that you are challenged to the core.

YOU NOW

WHAT WE LEARNED

We first addressed the damaging judgment that many of us have toward ourselves and recognized that we will be different, no matter how subtly, once we become post-Menopausal.

We looked at the *prima donnas* of Menopause, our symptoms, how they connect to each other and which ones are at the centre of your experience, negatively impacting your day-to-day life. We identified symptom triggers and the chronology of a symptom event.

WHAT WE DID

We highlighted negative self-talk and the damaging effect of it. We agreed that all those 'shoulds' and 'have tos' no longer have a place, and sought to replace them with empathy, recognizing that 'the change' offers us a series of choices.

We identified your symptoms and established their interconnectedness, highlighting those at the centre that drive many of the others. You specified the impact of each on your life with a RAG (red, amber, green) table. Three reds against a symptom hit the 'impact reverse-jackpot'.

Once you identified your key symptom, you mapped the chronology of an event – when and how it shows up and what you do when it does. You then mapped backwards, identifying any triggers.

HOW THIS HELPS

Our negative self-talk all too frequently goes under the radar, yet it can have a considerable impact. Identifying it when it occurs enables you to stop being so mean to yourself and be empathetic and supportive. You are changing. It is a fact. It's only right that you are your first, and most important, coach.

Understanding what your symptoms are, how they drive others and which ones are most impactful lets you decide on your next steps. If you know which symptom to tackle, you can get on and do it and realize the greatest improvement for your effort in using your resources that are naturally depleted at this time.

Seeing the chronology of your symptoms removes the unpredictability and stress of an event.

If you know there are triggers, you can put strategies in place to avoid them. If you need help, you can ask for it, whether that be at work or home. If you can clearly identify the start of an event and the stages throughout, you can put strategies in place to mitigate or manage it, and your emotional and physical response to it. Remember, your reaction is your choice.

FUTURE YOU

WHAT WE LEARNED

The opportunity offered by Menopause is in the future, not in the past. Wishing for a relived youth is distracting, damaging and pointless. It probably wasn't quite as good as you remember it anyway! Recognizing where you are in key areas of life today and where you want to be, provides two important pieces of information. First, in our busy lives it is easy to lose sight of how we are actually living on a day-to-day basis – by putting a stake in the ground, we can clearly see for ourselves whether things are as we thought or hoped they would be. Second, by marking where we would like to be, we are priming ourselves for our five- and ten-year plan.

The five- and ten-year plan is a common planning tool. We used them to identify where we would like to be, what we would like to be doing and who we would like to be doing it with. We grounded them and made them achievable with small next steps.

The plans don't happen in isolation – achieving your five-year plan is the foundation for your ten-year plan; therefore, setting workable goals that inspire and draw us forward is essential. This plan, curated by you, for you, is a superpower. It will pull you forward even during the darkest of times. It has to be compelling. Pull strategies are always more effective than push – there is far less friction.

Last, we learned that self-care is vital at this time in our lives. It's time to review how we eat, the exercise we do or don't do, cut back on alcohol and quit smoking. It is time to see these adjustments in lifestyle as an advantage and a benefit rather than a loss. We are showing self-respect and doing exactly what the name says: caring for ourselves.

WHAT WE DID

We started by turning our focus firmly on the opportunities offered in the future, recognizing that the choices are ours to take.

We then identified where you are today in five key areas of life and where you would like to be. This led to your five-year plan, which specified where you would like to be, what you would like to be doing and with whom you would like to be doing it.

The ten-year plan is a further development of this, an extension. It recognizes that ten years is a long time during a period of such intense change and that your ambitions for yourself can similarly change radically. Given all of that, you defined how you would like your life to be.

HOW THIS HELPS

Being able to look forward with optimism at a future that is compelling and full of opportunity when all around you seems dark is a superpower. It is a positive lifeline. Everything flows, and you are never standing still.

Outside of this, you are shaping your ambitions for your career and personal relationships. The two plans will act as a foundation for all aspects of your life. They will help you create, develop and maintain relationships; they will underpin decisions and where you choose to place your focus and energies. For a small series of exercises, their impact can be considerable.

Keep the plans with you as you progress through the rest of the book – and beyond. They are a living, breathing intent. They will underpin and inform many of the choices you take as you progress through the next chapters in this book. You may find that they need amending or adapting. They are yours and are always open to change, but if something is important or of value, ensure that it is cherished throughout.

Now you must never lose sight of the future you.

Now that you're in much greater control of your relationship with yourself, let's see how we manage our relationships at work.

Part III

WORK

CHAPTER 16
YOUR WORK RELATIONSHIPS: INTRODUCTION

As a generation of women who have demanded an education, flooded universities and sought a career outside of the previously limited options of administration or the typing pool, we have changed the Western perception of our gender, our abilities and our potential. We faced and fought the sexism and racism of the 1980s, where derogatory behaviour was part of the wider social culture, yet #MeToo shows that there is much more still to do. Our generation are the rabble rousers, the fighters; we took the baton from our mothers and aunts who had demanded equal pay[13] and continued to change the law to protect and support us through pregnancy and maternity leave.[14] We punched through the false ceiling only to find a glass one in its place, and have continued to chip away at it, demanding transparency over gender pay, and greater gender balance on company boards. It's a continuing struggle.

Menopause is the last taboo for us as a society and the workplace has simply reflected the wider social perspective and discomfort. The degree of variability in women's experiences means Human Resources (HR) departments have struggled to manage and incorporate its extremes into an approach or policy that supports every woman's experience in a respectful and empathetic manner. Yet, with the introduction of guidelines and supporting documentation from the Chartered Institute of Personnel and Development[15] (CIPD) and the Faculty of Occupational Medicine (FOM), this highlights the growing recognition and importance of this phase of women's lives.

This chapter is all about recognizing that your Menopause does not stop at the security barrier and wait to be collected at the end of the day from some form of symptom crèche. We will look at your relationships at work in the three directions of the organizational hierarchy – upwards (your line manager), sideways (your colleagues and peers) and downwards (your team) – and having a Menopause conversation, making the most of the relationships over time, and what to do if they go wrong.

By the end of this chapter, you will understand your value in the workplace and the importance of remaining focused on your own ambitions. You will realize that conversation, openness and a little vulnerability are crucial to successfully maintaining both your working relationships and your career throughout your Menopause.

CHAPTER 17
CONTEXT: SOCIETY

◆

Relationships exist in context. We can't extract them and deal with them in the abstract. They change over time as their environment alters and are affected by your own decisions and the acts or omissions of others. We need to consider the influencing factors in this dynamic.

THE CHANGING EMPLOYMENT MARKET

There are good reasons professional bodies are showing an increasing interest in Menopause.

In just 20 years, there has been a 17% increase in the number of women in the workforce aged between 50 and 64, compared to a 12.2% increase in men of the same age.[16] This level of gender balancing is only set to rise.

More women are in the workforce and, in turn, more of us are in positions of seniority. We have longevity of service and decades of knowledge and experience within that service. Just as with men, as our careers peak, we are at our most valuable to our employers, not only in our day-to-day ability but also in our intrinsic understanding of how the industry, company and its culture work, both from a macro and micro perspective. With Menopause heralding a period of vulnerability and uncertainty for maturing female talent, recognition and flexibility on the part of the organization are key to retention.

Recruitment costs are currently estimated at 15–20% of the first year's salary. Add to this the investment in training and mentoring necessary during the onboarding process, and the cost can be considerable. Conversely, the loss of knowledge and experience in niche or key roles is a hidden yet substantial cost that is rarely discussed and difficult to quantify. The risks of losing women from the workforce at this time of their lives is very real; current estimates state that 10%[17] of women leave paid employment altogether due to Menopausal symptoms.

This is compounded by our social discomfort in discussing Menopause. Multiple surveys, including that by the Trades Union Congress (TUC)[18] show that over a fifth of women feel embarrassed speaking to their line managers about their Menopausal experience, and many managers feel discomfort at the prospect of having to discuss it. Interestingly, the same survey found that over half said the gender of their manager mattered.

The requirements for skills and qualifications is changing as technology has changed. New roles have appeared that didn't exist even ten years ago,[19] including specialists in social media, search engine optimization, podcasts, mobile apps and artificial intelligence. Attracting, retaining and developing the right people is, therefore, critical. It has been estimated that the over-50s now comprise almost one third of the working age population.[20] By 2022, 14.5 million more jobs will be created, but only 7 million younger workers will enter the workforce[21] – this represents a 7.5 million gap.

Finally, the balance of employment is changing with an increasing number of contingent (or 'gig') workers within most organizations. It is no longer a question of being full or part time. Contingent workers, which incorporate all temporary and contract staff, have risen from 15% of the workforce in 2014 to 20% in 2017.[22] This rise is likely to indicate an upward ongoing trend.

STEREOTYPES

We have numerous social and visual signposts for our expectations of people at varying times in their lives. This applies to both men and women.

In this regard, we assume that Menopause is an older woman's affliction – cue mental images of a woman in her 60s with a fan. Unfortunately, society still chooses to depict Menopausal women as older, stressed and sweaty. Women are generally more able to retain higher levels of health and fitness than in previous generations. Those in their 50s can easily appear a decade younger – and so media depiction takes no chances. It scales up for the avoidance of doubt. Blue rinse, twinset and pearls, therefore, defies misinterpretation.

Some of these are accurate but, as with any stereotype, the vast majority are not. By having these social stereotypes, we diminish and sideline the experience of those who do not fit our expectations. As a society, we have learned that mental illness can have no outward signs, and that it no longer fits the Victorian straight-jacketed asylum-bound images of our youth. Any one of us can suffer from mental illness – young, old, rich or poor – and it is the same for Menopause. Any woman can be experiencing it, even much earlier in her life than expected, and many will have a hard time. In reality, there is no such thing as a normal, uniform or standard Menopause, as discussed in Chapter 1; the only thing that is standard is the need to support women through this transitionary phase.

THE LEGISLATIVE FRAMEWORK

With all the cultural considerations taken into account, there are formal aspects to the relational context within UK legislation and the policies of organizations.

In the UK, the Equality Act (2010) incorporates age, sex and disability as three of nine core protected characteristics; employers are required to ensure that employees are not discriminated against in relation to these characteristics. Menopause, while not specifically stated, may be incorporated into the age, sex and disability categorizations. Organizations have a legal duty to provide reasonable adjustments for disabilities. But whether something amounts to a disability for the purposes of the Act is dependent on the severity, longevity and impact of a woman's symptoms on her day-to-day activities and is decided by a tribunal or court on a case-by-case basis. Therefore, it is not possible to say that Menopause is considered to be a disability, but that it *may* be depending on the individual circumstances.

While there is limited legal precedent to date, organizations are at risk of incurring the financial and reputational costs that come with a legal case for unfair or constructive dismissal, or on the grounds of discrimination by age, sex or disability, harassment and/or victimization, or a failure to provide reasonable adjustments specific to the symptoms of each woman.

It is important to note that discrimination can be both direct and indirect. Direct discrimination occurs when an individual is treated less favourably as a result of a protected characteristic. Indirect discrimination occurs when an organization operates a policy, criterion or practice that puts someone with a particular characteristic at a disadvantage to those without it. An example relating to Menopause could be an organization that has a policy prohibiting flexible working hours; this places women experiencing Menopause at a disadvantage, as they may need to work flexibly in order to cope with their symptoms.

Although there have been only a few cases so far, this is likely to be a developing area of law in the future. It is also important to note that there are no costs to the individual in bringing a claim to the employment tribunal; an individual can choose to represent themselves and it is free to lodge a claim.

In addition to discrimination, the Equality Act also prohibits harassment and victimization on the grounds of the same nine protected characteristics – bearing in mind that we referenced age, sex and disability previously. Harassment is unwanted conduct related to a relevant protected characteristic, which has the purpose or effect of violating an individual's dignity or creating an intimidating, hostile, degrading, humiliating or offensive environment for that individual.

The legislation defines victimization as taking place when someone is subjected to a detriment or is in some way penalized for raising a complaint. This would only arise if a woman had made a complaint about her treatment regarding her Menopause and was later treated less favourably, specifically in relation to this complaint.

In the event of a claim for discrimination, an organization would need to demonstrate that they had not treated someone less favourably or, in the case of disability discrimination, that they have made reasonable adjustment for the individual. If it had been brought on the grounds of disability, then it would be dependent on whether the woman's specific Menopausal symptoms met the definition of a disability. This would be the first stage of any legal case.

Discrimination or harassment can take place both formally and informally.

Formal discrimination is due to a breach of contractual requirements and corporate expectations. If people are not performing to their previously agreed targets, not working their agreed hours, or behaving in a way that is outside of the published expectations, then this is a formal matter and would be dealt with via an organization's policies and procedures into capability of performance. At the very least, an exploratory conversation will be arranged. The last part of this is the demonstration of the duty of care the organization has for its employees by offering appropriate adjustments to support them through recognized illnesses or issues.

In terms of Menopause specifically, an organization can choose to set these out in advance in a Menopause policy or guidance document to ensure that managers know what is expected of them. Of course, these can influence all of the points above.

The informal discrimination or harassment is harder to identify and establish, and potentially a creator of greater long-term damage. It is of particular importance to women of Menopausal age, as it places them in a position of vulnerability when they no longer fit into a culture characterized by features (for example) such as long hours, high levels of work-related stress from targets and expectations, and regular or high-intensity out-of-hours socializing. Women during Menopause manage none of these well.

Comments such as 'part-timer', 'half day today is it?' or 'going home early ... again?' are not helpful and could amount to harassment. In fact, they inveigle their way into the psyche of the receiver, often increasing levels of stress and magnifying symptoms. If a woman starts to go home on time instead of working a 40 to 50-hour week due to her symptoms, this is not working part time. Neither is it when she has agreed flexitime to help her manage anxiety or insomnia, nor if she has to leave earlier one day as she has run out of sanitary ware and clean clothes due to flooding.

Belittling women who can no longer drink or socialize perhaps as they used to is not helpful either and may also amount to harassment if this takes place in a work context. Just one glass of wine a night increases a woman's risk of developing breast cancer.[23] Alcohol also interferes with the absorption of vitamin D,[24] hence affecting bone density and placing women at an increased risk of developing osteoporosis. The risk of heart disease increases considerably in post-Menopausal women.[25] Eating rich food and drinking exacerbates this, as it does for obesity, which considerably increases the risk of numerous cancers for both women and men. These are very real health risks that women have to face. Changing your lifestyle to a healthier one is something that should be supported, not scorned publicly.

Direct or indirect harassment or victimization is unacceptable, and all reasonable employers should take steps to ensure that this does not occur in their organizations or, if it does, take appropriate action against perpetrators. They constitute outdated, uninformed and uneducated opinions, which could be extremely damaging to your organization's reputation. As they are cumulative, they are also less able to be identified specifically, as each example alone can appear trivial. Reporting a sustained campaign of abuse can be difficult in terms of gathering evidence and securing willing witnesses prepared to manage the consequences.

Of course, there is an interplay between both informal and formal, in that harassment often causes distress, which exacerbates symptoms and causes absenteeism and poor performance which, in turn, causes increased harassment. More worryingly, it is likely to trigger a performance management process such as capability or sickness management, which may, in turn, cause further distress. It is a downward zigzag as the victim is pinged, pinball like, from one side to the other.

Equality is a value that is fortunately increasing generally in the workplace. If you as a manager recognize any of this behaviour in your team or team culture, you have a duty of care to all your team to call it out and deal with it.

In having a comprehensive and empathetic Menopause policy or guidelines, which is easily and readily available and deployed, organizations will mitigate against legal action. It is in employers' interests to work with each woman in a flexible and supportive manner to ensure that she can stay within the workforce and retain her career, as well as ensure the working environment is free from discrimination and harassment.

There have been two successful employment tribunals in the UK.[26] However, as Menopause gains greater recognition within the workplace, it is increasingly likely that more cases will occur. Any legal action brought by employees against their employers is both financially and reputationally damaging.

FEMALE GATEKEEPERS

By gatekeepers, we mean those who stand between you and needed support.

For those in the thick of their Menopausal maelstrom, it is the greatest betrayal of all to have another woman, whom you have turned to for support, whether it be a friend, colleague or in some cases even a female GP, belittle you or dismiss your experience. Some are unaware, as they are yet to be Menopausal, but many are women who sailed through their own without a thought.

I am not of the belief that we are part of a bonded sisterhood – far from it. Women base their response to other women on their own experiences. This is evident when it comes to menstrual periods, having and raising children and Menopause. I have seen women roll their eyes at others, tell them to "just get on with it," "it's not that bad!" or to "stop making such a big deal of it" or even that they are "letting the female side down" fearing that a show of vulnerability weakens the gender.

In many respects, we all do it. For example, I didn't know how hard it was to be a parent until I was one. At which point I was suddenly able to empathize. And herein lies the point. Women who are having a hard time deserve empathy. This is not something that they have chosen, and they don't deserve your judgment. We can't expect others to open the gates to support if we can't or don't. We all need to open the gates when asked. It is about human kindness and has little to do with gender.

CHAPTER 18
CONTEXT: THE ORGANIZATION

We should always bear in mind that we are thrown together with those with whom we work and are asked to make the best of it. Our work relationships are an accident of circumstance. Very often it's more accidental than that. People are often organized into groups based on availability and/or business skill, by those who don't know them.

THE WORKPLACE DYNAMIC

More than in any other environment we shall cover, relationships in the workplace exist in a complex and interdependent environment. At the top of the triangle[27] is *what* we do – the nature of the work we do and the opportunities we have to learn and grow. To the left are the social relationships of the workplace – *why* we do what we do, *how* we do it and *who* with (at every level). At the bottom right is *where* we do it, the physical spaces we inhabit.

This dynamic affects our relationships in obvious and not-so-obvious ways, in that sometimes we'll know who or what has caused an event and other times we won't.

This dynamic drives the emergence of stress, an increasing problem in the workplace. A report by the CIPD in the UK[28] cited the two main causes of stress as work overload and your line manager. Yes, the same line manager you may need to have a conversation with about your Menopause.

Bear in mind, too, that the workplace dynamic means that relationships will either be getting better or getting worse. Whichever way, they are never static and are in a state of constant flux. You need to recognize the direction that each relationship is moving in. The strategies we will develop will ensure we focus on them getting better.

THE CULTURAL LANDSCAPE

Workplace culture is hard to define – so we'll stick with 'how we do things around here'. Of course, culture is impacted by the societal factors mentioned, people changes and what the organization is focusing on (cost savings, investments, expanding, mergers and acquisitions). At the point in time your Menopause occurs, it is important in the context of relationships at work to understand the environment and dynamics around you and where you are within it. This will affect the way you discuss Menopause and the development of your relationships while it takes it course.

Much of an organization's culture is defined by the stories we tell one another. To change a culture can take considerable time.

It is worth evaluating your organization's culture. It will help define the approach you take to your relationships. Quite clearly when using the scale on the next page, in which a mark close to 1 is poor and to 5 is high, the more the pattern is to the left, the more effort is likely to be required. It may also be that when you stand back and consider the organization's culture, you question whether it's a place you want to be, especially with Menopause approaching or present.

Connect the line through the marks – you want to be to the right-hand side of the diagram. Take care to consider those areas where the marks are toward the left – you may need to consider how you deal with your work relationships where organizational culture may not be on your side.

Inclusive

1	2	3	4	5

Balanced

1	2	3	4	5

Understanding

1	2	3	4	5

Patient

1	2	3	4	5

Accommodating

1	2	3	4	5

Development-oriented

1	2	3	4	5

Long-term

1	2	3	4	5

Flexible (hours, location)

1	2	3	4	5

Work/life balanced

1	2	3	4	5

Output-oriented[29]

1	2	3	4	5

MANAGEMENT CULTURE

The degree to which an organization values the skills of good management as a discipline will be demonstrated in the level of investment and training provided to both new and established managers. Historically, managers have often been promoted into their roles due to functional excellence (they're good at what they *do*), which can be unrelated to the skills associated with enabling people to be the best they can be. In our particular context, we also often underestimate the pastoral skills needed by good managers – being able to spot when someone is struggling and offer support.

The well known Peter Principle[30] highlights that people are often promoted above their level of competence. While the strategy of promotion based on existing skill or meritocracy has its advantages, a good organization recognizes shortcomings and provides ongoing training in what are considered softer, yet seemingly more complex, skills to learn.

This is not to say that you won't find a good manager inside an organization that does not take this approach, but that will be more by accident or fortune than design. It does, however, mean that you stand a better chance of having a productive conversation if you are within what we might call a 'management-positive' organization.

POLITICS

Despite what organizations say about working together, collaborating and being team-focused (with no 'I'), almost all manage people as individuals – contracts, pay, benefits, promotion, status, recognition, accolades, you name it.

Organizations are, by nature, a collection of self-interested egos, however much we are engaged or have a sense of common purpose. On this basis, everyone has a personal agenda. Some are stronger and more amoral than others. Yet every organization is riven with politics. The difficulty at the time of Menopause is that politically others may seek to take advantage. You've never needed the stress from continual positioning and posturing, and you need it less than ever now – but by the same token, denying it isn't helpful.

This necessitates a relationships strategy based on openness and honesty – having the conversations, drawing others to you for support, working with your managers, colleagues and team in ways that set the politics aside and neutralize its potentially harmful effects.

POLICIES AND PROCEDURES

The effectiveness of an organizational policy depends entirely on how it is written. A well-crafted and comprehensive policy will act as a formal framework for any conversation about it in the workplace and will help with creating and maintaining relationships. Every woman approaching Menopause should familiarize themselves with their organization's policy.

Sometimes Menopause provisions are made within a broader-based policy reflecting the comparative immaturity of recognition of this phase of a woman's life. An entire absence of any referral would be extremely disappointing and, if identified, should be raised officially immediately.

If you do have one, it's important in the UK that it is in line with the latest guidelines from the CIPD and FOM. This being the case, make sure you are aware of what Menopause is, how it affects women both in work and outside of it, and lastly, what employers are doing to support women through this transitionary phase.

The next step is to be aware of what your organization is offering in the way of temporary adjustments, coaching and flexible working hours. Please note, none of these are unusual.

THE IMPORTANCE OF WELLBEING

Employee wellbeing has become an increasingly important feature of organizational life over the past ten years. While many organizations have historically covered most aspects of a wellbeing strategy within their people and workplace policies and provisions, they were, until the last five years, seldom drawn together as a distinct and tangible programme.

Menopause has a justifiable claim to be included in a wellbeing strategy, given its breadth of coverage across the workforce, impact and longevity. Within many wellbeing frameworks – usually comprising seven or eight domains – Menopause has not been easy to place, due to the lack of uniformity previously discussed. For the individual, the wellbeing focus spreads across the physical, occupational, psychological, spiritual and economic domains. For the organization, the environmental, social and cultural domains are of most importance. Most organizations, for simplicity and ease of implementation, usually focus on areas that have clearly defined parameters, for example pregnancy; however, the variability of Menopause poses a more complex challenge.

The Employee Value Proposition (EVP), defining why a specific company considers itself an employer of choice, carries considerable weight in recruitment, and a wellbeing framework that incorporates Menopause is a key part of this. As previously mentioned, no organization wants the negative publicity associated with legal action; it damages their ability to both recruit and retain staff. Good employees vote with their feet.

When we explore conversations with your manager a little later, it's a useful part of the planning exercise to consider the measures you would like to see in place against each of the domains of the wellbeing wheel. It can help you organize your thoughts.

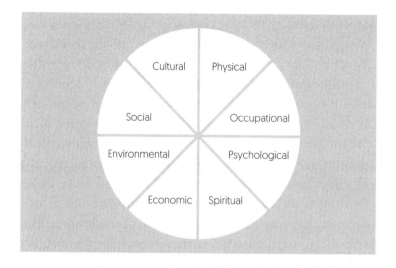

A RATINGS SOCIETY

We are a society obsessed with ratings – instant evaluation is ubiquitous. We have all seen the faces on the simple dashboards at airports. The company that created them, HappyOrNot, continues to attract massive investment, because they work.[31] Employers are rated, too, and the employee experience is now open source, much discussed on general social media platforms and those specifically related, such as Glassdoor. Positive and negative experiences are immediately conveyed and generally available.

If an organization has a positive or negative attitude toward Menopause, the chances are that everyone interested will know about it. That means if your Menopause is approaching, you have research at your fingertips to suggest whether your current or a prospective employer is likely to take your condition seriously.

CHAPTER 19
YOU AT WORK

A DEEP BREATH

You're a professional with a reputation you have worked and struggled for.

You may have had an unblemished career spanning two or three decades, yet within months of Menopause beginning, your confidence could diminish. You are repeatedly late, not concentrating, forgetting important information or appointments, bursting into tears at random, getting annoyed with people over trivial matters, rushing out of meetings and presentations – all behaviours that were previously unheard of and certainly not considered 'corporate' or 'professional'.

I will call on you to remember the work that you did in Chapter 3 and Chapter 9, defining and understanding your symptoms, their interconnectedness and their chronology, and to remind you of the steps you defined to manage your responses and lastly, to keep in mind your five- and ten-year plan. Those ambitions will draw you forward when the proverbial hits the fan.

Seeking support is at the centre of managing your working relationships during your Menopause. You can't hide your Menopause and, if you are one of the three quarters of women experiencing symptoms, it's likely you can't deal with it alone. For many women, it doesn't come naturally, especially given the extra effort required on this side of the gender divide to create a successful career. Add to this the sense of isolation many women feel, and it can be a very big ask indeed. Ensuring that you keep positive relationships with those you work with will enable you to foster empathy from others and create the necessary narrative you will need to thrive.

You are not asking for anything extraordinary; you are stating that you value your career and your working relationships and would like some temporary adjustments to help you continue with it.

Remember, too, that at some juncture you are going to be on the other side of the Menopause conversation – as a manager, colleague or member of a team – when another woman will be talking to you about her symptoms and seeking support. You will just as likely be a giver of support as a receiver of it.

YOUR WHOLE SELF

There is now much talk about bringing your whole self to work, a prospect that was unheard of less than a decade ago. In this regard, it is assumed we no longer have to dispense with aspects of our personality and character when we move through the revolving door every morning, but can be our full selves.

There has been a considerable change in perspective on human fragility and vulnerability. Studies such as Google's Project Aristotle[32] and Amy Edmondson's work, among others, have focused on the importance of 'psychological safety' – a space for safe conflict, where we can express ourselves among our colleagues without fear of judgment or worse. There is, of course, the work that Brené Brown has done on vulnerability.[33] While not specific to the workplace, it is equally applicable.

Bringing our whole self during Menopause means bringing all our symptoms and the changes they entail, too.

All of this points to the fact that we should be able to have Menopause conversations at work and neither these nor what we suffer from be held against us. They depict a supportive and understanding environment in which we can speak frankly and honestly. In many respects, however, Menopause tests the boundaries of these ideas. We can't assume it's all in place. You will still encounter attitudes that suggest you can leave the Menopausal aspects of your whole self at home, no need to bring them with you.

GO AWAY, I'M HAVING A CAREER

There have been many steps along the way here. You probably started out at the bottom of the pile, had Saturday jobs, stocked shelves, pulled pints or watered plants at the local garden centre. You have striven, kept focused and worked all hours to keep progressing. You have shown commitment and deserve all the recognition you have achieved. It's likely you were lining up a major push to the next level of achievement, whether that be management, a new job or starting a new business. That ladder that was difficult enough to climb has become, with the unwelcome arrival of your Menopause, a rather slippery pole.

For those among us who have been in control of our life experience to date – and to be honest, our career is often the area where we have micromanaged the outcome at every level – this can be extremely disconcerting. Where working harder and smarter has delivered success, suddenly those skills are rendered ineffective against the symptom onslaught. It can feel as though you are drifting in a very choppy sea without a rudder, a sail or an engine.

"Why can't I control this, why can't I make it go away?" is a common request. Obviously, this train of thought damages your self-esteem and your confidence which, in association, magnifies and intensifies the impact of your symptoms. You have not chosen this course and, therefore, controlling your symptoms is not your choice either. How you respond to them, however, is.

JOB CIRCUMSTANCES

Your circumstances add complexity to the challenge, too.

It is extremely common for women to lose all confidence in their abilities due to brain fog, loss of short-term memory and verbal recall. You open your mouth to say something and there is nothing there. No words, no alternatives, just a blank. This is shocking if you are normally a skilled wordsmith with perfect comedic timing. The joke is often on you at that point.

If you work in an environment where keeping your cool is essential, hot flushes are your worst enemy. For example, if you're a pilot or a surgeon, where the public require you to appear unflustered and untouched by stress, how can you remain authoritative when you are sweating it out every ten minutes with a face the colour of a beetroot? The physical response is, of course, a contradiction to everything we perceive is required.

If your work means that you cannot leave your post or working environment even for a short time, a continuous need to wee due to stress or urge incontinence is excruciating. This symptom can affect all women, not just those who had babies via a vaginal birth, due to the drop in oestrogen.

HAVE YOU BEEN HERE BEFORE?

You may have had children – remember how that challenge felt to your career? Menopause can feel like the second cycle of career disappointment.

You've been through it – pregnancy slowing you down, maternity leave, early years flexibility, a decade of disturbed sleep, the spiralling costs of childcare, illness announced on the morning of a vital meeting. It could be that just as your children are entering high school and starting to show enough independence to allow you to kick on with your career, Menopause hits. It's no wonder you feel cursed.

By the same token, looking at it positively, you got through it. Raising children is far tougher than the adverts have you believe. You've faced down the irrational and often spiteful prejudice before. You are now geared and programmed for struggle. Yet you were resourceful, strong and determined, and you wonder how you ever coped with vomit down the back of your best killing-it cashmere jacket. But you did. And that resourcefulness will stand you in good stead for this phase of your life. It's good to realize that there is some payback.

FINANCES

If you find talking about money uncomfortable, you need to get over it. You are a grown woman.

Your focus on maintaining your career and your current and future roles is not just about your self-esteem. One of the key reasons we work is to earn money. While we would like to live our best life, we also need to pay the mortgage, feed and clothe ourselves and our dependents, help pay for our ageing parents' growing care costs and, with whatever is left, buy the things that make it feel worthwhile – like holidays. And, of course, shoes or handbags.

The other less talked about reason we work is to create a pension for when we get older. The pensionable age is increasing across the developed world, which means that by the time many of us reach it, we will be at least seven years older than previous generations would have been. While this can be discouraging, it does give most of us an opportunity to plug the deficit.

Your ability to provide for your later years is a key part of work remuneration. Pay into your pension, and you will be grateful you did. If you have 20 years' continuous service with your organization, it is likely that you will be one of the last lucky few to have a final salary pension. This should be protected at all costs. In addition to the importance of retaining it, it also means that climbing the ladder becomes doubly more valuable with every rung you heave yourself onto.

The final reason to focus on retaining your current earning potential is shares. If you are lucky enough to earn them as part of your package or that you can save toward them as part of a company scheme, the windfall potential is considerable. They can be rainy day money, or they can be life-changing.

Money is an important part of why we work. It is also an important reason you are investing the effort to maintain and develop your working relationships.

STEPPING OFF

Menopause can feel like a conveyor belt to the abyss.

Yet you have already given yourself the means to step off. You have identified your symptoms, their interconnectedness, their severity and their impact. You have mapped their chronology and identified triggers. Most importantly of all, you have given yourself some strategies for how to do this.

Look back over the latter part of **You Now** and there is your own solution, your tailor-made strategy. If you need to amend it in any way or tweak it, feel free; it's a living, breathing plan, and it will be impacted by a huge array of factors. As discussed previously, the sense of control you will gain from having this in place will empower you. Your response is within your power to manage.

Once you have a grip on things, take a look at your five- and ten-year plans. Borrow from your post-Menopausal future self. Perhaps close your eyes and step into how that feels, explore every sensory detail. Even an inkling of how good that feels will help you manage your relationships. Because manage, you will.

CHAPTER 20
YOUR SYMPTOMS AT WORK

You're in a captive environment with people you haven't chosen to be with – and now no matter how much of your 'whole self' you bring to work, and their whole selves your colleagues bring, suddenly your physiology changes beyond your control. Much of managing your relationships at work will be down to your symptoms – recognizing them, talking about them and managing them. You may have to talk about flooding with someone with whom you've not even mentioned your athlete's foot to.

I have covered the four most debilitating and embarrassing symptoms at work that are likely to feature in any discussions. I have also reiterated some of the mitigation suggested earlier in the book, in case of skimming. I know, we all do it.

THE SYMPTOMS PUZZLE

As we have discussed, Menopause symptoms are wide-ranging, unique to the individual and change over time. Therefore, it is likely as you manage your relationships at work that others will attempt to establish other non-Menopausal causes of your symptoms. Some may even attribute them to a lack of commitment. By doing this, they are undermining your experience and questioning your character. It is a tricky situation to defend and justify. You shouldn't need to, but you may find you have to.

Your hot flushes may be the result of a bad diet, your anxiety may be workload-related, your sleeplessness due to a wild, secret social life. This is why Chapter 1 of this book should not be read lightly – it's vital in any discussion at work, enabling you to articulate and explain your symptoms.

ANXIETY AND DEPRESSION

At a time when workplace stress and mental health are recognized like never before, which is significantly a welcome progress, we add the complication of Menopause and its causal link with depression.

If you have suffered from depression at any time in your life, there is a greater likelihood that you will experience depression during Menopause.[34] There is also a link between migraines with aura and Menopausal depression.[35] Lastly, you might have neither of these yet still experience depression during Menopause. As hormone imbalance is not the same as depression, I strongly advise you to seek advice from your GP or a registered British Menopause Society specialist to determine whether HRT will help or resolve this before you think about taking antidepressants. In the UK, this facility is available on the NHS, but while you will need to wait a few months to be seen, they are amazing when you do. Suicide in women is at its highest during the Menopausal years.

In addition to this, self-care is important. If you find yourself sinking because you aren't sleeping enough or are stressed, step back and take the time you need. It's like they say in the safety presentation on aeroplanes, place your own mask over your face before helping others. You are your first priority; you are at your most able and effective when you are well. Take this symptom very seriously.

SLEEP DEPRIVATION

Lack of sleep will exacerbate stress and lead to lapses in concentration at work (some lengthy) and irritability as your fuse shortens in proportion to the reduced hours of recuperation. Therefore, lack of sleep will directly impact your relationships at work. You will be able to work around some of the interactions, but not all, and your guard will drop.

If night sweats are the issue, stick to natural fabrics on the bed and on you. If you wear nightclothes, keep them light, simple and made of silk or cotton. There are new fabrics coming onto the market that claim to keep you cool, too.

If you drink coffee, tea or alcohol, these can exacerbate this symptom. Try going caffeine - and alcohol - free for a month or two and see if this helps.

Lastly, magnesium was my saviour.[36] It helped me drift off to sleep; if I didn't take it, it often meant I didn't sleep. As with any supplement, always seek professional advice before taking it.

MEMORY LOSS

This symptom is incredibly common and difficult to manage, especially for those who have to stand up in front of others and speak. The horror of opening your mouth to say something important, only to find that all memory of the sentence or the point you were about to make has gone completely is haunting and very real.

The other side of this is simply forgetting things, things you said you would do, appointments, events; they simply drop out of your mind, never to return, or if they do it's to remind you that you have forgotten, after the event. You must write things down and, of course, *remember* to write them down. Your life is about to become listed.

FLOODING

This is messy and embarrassing and probably the most potentially difficult symptom to have to discuss with anyone at work. Most men and a large percentage of women have never heard the expression outside of climate change. As the name denotes, it is incredibly heavy and often unpredictable bleeding. Because of its intensity, it drenches clothing, bedding, mattresses and furniture within an embarrassingly short period of time.

Managing this symptom can be very difficult, in particular for those who do a lot of travelling for business. If you have long flights and are staying in hotels, there is little chance of having protective covers on the bed, in the aeroplane or the hotel. Sanitary ware of the most robust nature is your first call, as is carrying clean clothing.

When travelling for business, ensure that wherever you stay there are laundry facilities. It is not something you should have to do, but the unpredictable and intense nature of this symptom requires thought and planning. If you suffer from this symptom, you should speak to your GP, as there may be other options available to you.

INCONTINENCE

Close in nature to flooding, women agonize over their inability to stop themselves from weeing, with the resulting smell and the huge embarrassment of wet clothing. Suddenly, your involuntary control deserts you.

Mitigating this requires pelvic floor exercises. Your GP surgery has access to specialist physiotherapists who can work wonders in this regard. Failing this, there are an array of gadgets on the market that will help you do the exercises, along with numerous videos on the internet. As with any exercise, for it to be effective you must do them every day. In addition to this, your GP can also prescribe local (vaginal) oestrogen cream.

HOT FLUSHES

Finally, the mother of all Menopause symptoms, the driver of stereotypes, punchline of prejudice, yet still entirely misunderstood by anyone not having suffered from them. The distress of a sudden and unannounced hike in body temperature with associated sweating and reddening of the face cannot be underestimated, especially when face to face with a work colleague during an important conversation. Or, heaven forbid, an interview.

There are some practical ways to deal with the effects – but unfortunately, we can't hit the pause button when it comes upon us.

You need a tactic to bring your temperature down quickly. The common suggestion is to wear clothing in layers. This does not mean a cardigan and the ubiquitous pearls.

Fold and store all your long-sleeve tops and dresses; desperately trying to roll up a tight-sleeved top when you are clammy is simply not going to happen. Anything silk needs to be stored as well, as it shows sweaty marks terribly and clings. Linen is another fabric that works against you; by the time you have had a couple of hot flushes, you will look like you have slept on a park bench in your very expensive suit. Whenever possible, avoid man-made fibres that don't breathe and act like a dustbin liner. Also avoid any clothing that needs dry cleaning that sits next to the skin of your upper body.

Get yourself a range of light jackets that you can wear over short-sleeve tops that act like a cardigan but make you feel more on top of your game. If you manage people, meetings or events, you need to feel that your clothes support you in your role, not compete with your symptoms to make you feel crap.

If you wear a uniform, this can be a complex area to tackle. With my work in the National Health Service (NHS) I have found that many members of staff are still expected to wear thick, heavily starched uniforms as well as tights. There are many industries where this is still the case. Women worry about odour and discolouration as well as discomfort (this is applicable for flooding and incontinence as well). Request access to breathable-fabric uniforms and a greater number than the usual two or three offered. Many women in these roles are the public face of their employer and, as such, should be supported in looking and feeling comfortable and confident in the clothes allocated to them.

Fans are a must and incredibly effective. I don't mean those horrible little plastic battery-operated things that just move the warm air around a bit and get caught in your hair. I mean those beautiful, elegant versions used by women for centuries. If you can't find one or don't have one at hand, make one by folding a piece of paper backwards and forwards, like you did at school. They work just as well.

Then there is makeup. Sweating continuously plays havoc with your skin and makeup. Anything powdery gets caught in your creases while the rest slides off your face. Invest in something light and durable. It will stay in place and help you feel professional. All eye makeup should be waterproof; otherwise, you will find that you look like a panda. The concern you will see on other people's faces will not be because you are sweating, but because they are wondering if you have either been crying or fighting. Or both.

We've covered a lot of the context for good reason – the more we understand about the environment in which we are conducting our relationships, the easier it is to plan for their development. We're ready now to look at the specifics – your manager, your colleagues and your team.

CHAPTER 21
YOUR MANAGER

Unless you work in an organization that embraced a new organizational structure such as holacracy, with its decentralized management and self-organizing teams, you will have a line manager.

Like it or not, your line manager is your judge. They set your objectives (hopefully in association with you), rate your performance and attitude, and hold the key to your advancement – or not. Therefore, they affect your self-esteem, pay, levels of stress and lifestyle. Just at the point you develop a positive relationship with them, you could end up with a new one and have to start all over again.

Sometimes no matter what you invest, you just won't be able to develop or even manage your relationship with your line manager – something will be chemically or spiritually wrong.

ASKING FOR [AND GETTING] SUPPORT

It is an unfortunate fact that colleagues, managers and employers quickly forget the decades of a woman's experience and great work when faced with a woman who outwardly, at least, no longer matches their expected or assumed code of behaviour. They begin not to recognize you, and you begin not to recognize yourself.

If you are taking sick leave as and when you need it, turning up late or going home early because you feel terrible, your absence will come under scrutiny. You could very quickly find yourself being called into a conversation that signifies the start of a disciplinary process. It may affect you materially or your promotion prospects. At worst, you could find yourself under performance management and in extreme cases, exited from the company. As a rule of thumb, it takes ten times the amount of time to rid the resulting prejudice than to create it.

Silence on your part creates a barrier. All your manager can see is that you are behaving unusually. Over time, this can morph into resentment on their part that you are not doing what they believe you should. This growing gap in perception can cause permanent damage to your relationships unless you begin to build the bridge of understanding by being open and being prepared to have the 'M' conversation.

There is a very big caveat here, and one which many women do not fully appreciate. If you don't actually declare that your symptoms are specifically associated with Menopause then, due to a lack of telepathy skills, your employer will most likely not understand and will not be able to connect the dots between changes in behaviours and what is actually going on. This is even more the case when you have an early Menopause, due to POI or a medically induced Menopause. While the first is difficult enough, the latter two can and most commonly are even more so.

The other point is that without formally declaring that you are going through Menopause, the law cannot protect you. At this point, you will need to put on your big girl pants and have the 'M' conversation – choose the path that appears easiest, as both will need to be brought into the loop eventually.

This is a big ask for many women and, therefore, a major stumbling block. In a survey conducted by the TUC,[37] one third of women reported that they suffered embarrassment or difficulties discussing their Menopause with their employer. This is not surprising given that the same number stated that they had experienced management criticism of Menopause-related sick leave. The latter is absolutely why you need to have this conversation, to ensure you are protected if things don't go as you would hope. Essentially, start the process. From here there is no going back.

You have had more difficult conversations than this. The difference is that this is personal. But it is important to recognize why you are doing this. You are respecting and valuing the effort and commitment you have shown to get this far. You are recognizing the importance of your salary and ultimately your pension, on yours and potentially your family's lifestyle and those who depend on you, whether that be children, elderly parents or both. Lastly, only you know the part this job plays in achieving your five and ten-year plan. All these things need to be focused on. You might find yourself squirming in your seat but change your focus – this is a vital step.

It is important to note that, legally, it is likely that you will need to get corroboration from your GP or gynaecologist that you are Menopausal (whichever of the three phases) and that you are suffering from specific symptoms. It is important that you request that any sick leave you take, due to Menopausal symptoms, be categorized as an ongoing health issue and not as a series of short-term absences.

In most organizations, you don't have to speak to your manager if you don't want to. You can request to speak to a manager once removed, HR or occupational health. This is not the case, however, for everyone, which means preparation is the key. Before you book your meeting, it's important to do some planning so that you are fully prepared and able to get the most out of your conversation.

IS YOUR MANAGER OPEN TO
THE 'M' CONVERSATION?

You've assessed the culture within your organization, as advised earlier in this chapter. When chatting in the lunch queue or around the tea point, do you compare notes on how others are coping and, importantly, how the manager or the organization are supporting them?

I spoke to a woman recently who holds a senior role in her organization. She and her team work hard and have a high expectation of professionalism and commitment. Much of what she said about winning contracts and working to deadlines will be familiar to many. What's not so familiar is how positively she spoke about her manager and his genuine care for those who work for him. I asked if she would be happy to have the 'M' conversation with him. Very quickly she said yes. Even in our short exchange, she had signposted many instances when her manager had responded positively to the needs of his staff and identified many attributes that made him approachable.

Are there stories told that indicate your manager has empathy? Perhaps displaying care or consideration for others, a recognition that those who work for them are complete human beings with complex lives, who occasionally need a little additional support? These are important stories. They build trust and cohesion, and they also tell you that the person you are going to speak to will be receptive. Before you proceed, think about any instances small or large that indicate that you can approach them on this subject.

Realistically, there should be no difference whether you are approaching a female or male line manager. The conversation needs to take place, the content needs to be consistent, and you can reasonably expect understanding and a plan from either. This isn't a case of it being a women's issue and, therefore, needing a woman to be the other party.

THE ART OF A SUCCESSFUL 'M' CONVERSATION AT WORK

It would seem extremely unfair that, along with having to manage the hurly burly of Menopause and all its associated symptoms, you are the one who has to broach the subject. The point to make here is that it's perfectly acceptable to request some temporary adjustments to support you through these transitionary years. Before you do, it's time to deploy some of the skills you utilize to do your job – don't park them in front of your computer and hope for the best.

DO YOUR HOMEWORK

Does your employer have any form of Menopause policy? If not, do they have policies relating to factors that may be personally debilitating for a period – such as long-term illness or mental health – that might be a benchmark? Menopause is not and never will be an illness, so it shouldn't be sitting here, but it may have been placed there in a less-enlightened time and needs to be drawn out, and the response the organization sets out in such circumstances may at least fit how you are feeling and what you need to happen.

As mentioned, in the UK the CIPD and FOM have some great materials readily available online that will provide you with an understanding of the basics both for you and your organization. This is the minimum that they should be offering.

WHAT'S YOUR DESIRED OUTCOME?

What do you want to walk away with from this conversation? Do you want greater understanding, specific adjustments or general awareness? If you are clear in your own mind about what you are looking for, you can guide the conversation in that direction. Be clear with yourself about what you need and what would be useful to have. If you have examples of when and how adjustments have been made for others either during Menopause or a bout of illness as discussed above, you can use these as a precedent for equal consideration. If nothing else, it shows that you are prepared and committed to surfacing from this positively.

On the next page is a table to write down your most troublesome symptoms. Then in the next column, note what adjustments you would like from your employer. The first four rows are examples of possible symptoms and potential adjustments, the rows thereafter are for you to fill in. Be proactive. Even if the adjustments aren't entirely agreed upon, you've started.

Here are some examples:

Symptom	Possible Adjustment
Anxiety, depression and panic attacks	Flexitime, working from home, quiet room to retreat to
Hot flushes	A fan, access to cold water and cooler seating areas, opportunities to leave the building and get fresh air, breathable uniforms, opportunity to wear trousers instead of tights. Multiple spare uniforms so that women can change during the day (applicable to flooding and incontinence as well)
Insomnia	Flexitime, working from home
All symptoms	Free onsite specialist coaching plus access to specialist medical advice and support
...	...
...	...
...	...

GET PROFESSIONAL BACKUP

You may not need to do this, as you could have an employer who can see that you are not as you used to be and is proactive in supporting staff. However, if you do not, I suggest you visit your GP and discuss your symptoms with them. It is irrefutable evidence if your Doctor has confirmed in writing that you are Menopausal and suffering from troubling symptoms.

If things are a little further along, and HR has started to flag that you are taking an unusual amount of sick leave or are demonstrating unusual behaviours, you may want to make this your priority.

CHOOSE WHO YOU ARE
GOING TO SPEAK TO

If you don't feel comfortable having this conversation with your manager, then choose somebody you do feel comfortable with. You want a constructive conversation, not awkward silence. This helps no one. As mentioned, you can speak to HR, occupational health or a manager once removed.

Go back to the earlier subsections and think about who would not only be empathetic, but would also be able to help you. You are looking for effective support via reasonable adjustments, not just a chat with tea and biscuits. You want a definable outcome.

The next step is to approach them to ask for a meeting. Give a brief outline of what this is about, because it's likely that they will need to do some preparation and homework as well. Again, you want to get the most out of this meeting, not build yourself up only to find you must do it all over again once they have had a chance to seek advice. If they don't feel able to have a conversation like this and defer to someone else, don't be perturbed – remain focused on your desired outcome.

FIND A QUIET SPACE FOR
THE CONVERSATION

You'll feel significantly better about the conversation if you're not interrupted or overheard. This isn't always possible in a modern workplace, so you may have to book a meeting room. The other aspect of this is that you are letting your manager know that this is both important and personal. Lastly, by defining where you have the meeting, you are creating a condition based on your terms. If you don't like certain rooms, don't book them. Make sure you are psychologically and physically comfortable before you begin.

MAP THE SCENARIOS

This is the final piece of planning prior to your meeting. Think about what you want to say and what they might say. Anticipate outcomes and eventualities. Map them – what you might say and they might say. This sounds like overkill, but if you run through potential scenes now, it will help you manage the outcome. Let's face it: if everything was OK, you wouldn't be here.

Recognize that you are not the person who may have been able to handle this conversation before your Menopause – you now have a propensity to emotional outbursts, forgetting things or withdrawing into yourself, to name but a few examples – so give yourself a chance. Running through scenarios removes a layer of stress and surprise, both of which are the clarion call for hot flushes, blank thoughts, emotional outbursts and anxiety. The more you hope these symptoms don't arise, the greater the chance they'll appear unannounced.

SET A REVIEW DATE

Menopause is a journey that potentially incorporates a quarter of your career. During this time, your symptoms may well change along the way. Because of this, it's important to recognize that if they do, your requirements at work will change as well. Agree on a review date before you finish your meeting, and book the meeting and venue – that way, you set the expectation that things might change. Add the caveat that if they do, you will arrange an additional meeting to address any issues promptly. While this may feel counterintuitive, it really is in your best interests to flag any issues early – that way, you are in control of the narrative.

We will assume from here that, awkward as it may have been, you have had the conversation and that Menopause is out in the open, understood and acknowledged, and that a plan for adjustments is in place. This, however, is just the start of the journey, the reset of the relationship based on a new mutually recognized reality.

MAINTAINING THE RELATIONSHIP

Your Menopause will change over time and, therefore, the response will need to as well. The relationship that has been developed with the Menopause discussion – possibly the most open and candid you have ever been with your manager – needs to be maintained.

While you may not be in the best condition for this, be clear about the expectations from their perspective. That is, workload, deliverables and presence in the office, balanced with the level of support you need to achieve all or some of it. The empathy needs to work both ways. Your manager is likely to be reliant on you to say what you need. It may be that you have skills or experience no one else has. You may lead a large team and your absence may expose your manager to increased day-to-day responsibility.

Transparency is a critical part of this process. It helps no one if you say you are going to deliver something by a specific date, and then the day before it is due, declare you won't. This is particularly so when you and your work are part of an interdependent series of activities. This can be complex and costly for an organization to resolve and will, therefore, damage your reputation and your ongoing relationship with your line manager. Being brutally frank is critical.

Be clear about what is and isn't possible for you at this point in time and why. It will give them an understanding of the challenges you face and why you may, at a future time, require additional or different support. However, try to be as practical as possible, achieving as much as you can with the minimal impact on performance and output. The more you show willingness and understanding, the greater opportunity over time to build trust.

It's tough to admit you're feeling like crap, but it's even tougher to admit that others think you're crap due to your own inactions.

Once this process begins, be prepared to become your own personal assistant. Make detailed notes of what was said and agreed, when and by when. It is vital that you have a record in case someone becomes malicious or decides to pursue a personal agenda that places you at a disadvantage. Sharing the notes of your key interactions will not only keep them abreast of progress but inform them that you mean business and that your professional persona is still in charge.

WHAT TO DO IF IT DETERIORATES

Sadly, in some instances, relations do deteriorate. It would be naïve to believe this was not the case or that one good conversation could resolve everything.

You have both a formal avenue and an informal avenue.

Formally, reacquaint yourself with your organization's Menopause policy. Identify any areas where your manager and their expectations may not have been in alignment. If this is the case, you are within your rights to speak to HR. You will need clear evidence – this is where your notes come in – of when things didn't go as they should have or as was agreed (and documented) between you. A confrontation is not constructive behaviour, but a planned, well-thought-through discussion is.

Follow the steps listed previously to help you prepare.

Informally, you always have the option of the 'off the record' conversation. You could, if the situation had deteriorated significantly, formally request that it is 'without prejudice', which means that legally it never happened and can't ever be quoted. This is a situation where you don't take any notes. Simply the process of requesting either changes the playing field. We are saying there is something wrong that needs putting right; we are being clear on the opportunity. You're less constrained, but don't believe that because something isn't recorded or 'didn't happen' that it, well, didn't happen. It will be remembered. However, it does allow you to clear the air. It's usually worth trying it off the record before on it.

This is also the time for some home truths. If you have missed agreed-upon deadlines, not turned up to work when you said you would, been unpleasant to colleagues or exhibited a multitude of other behaviours driven by your symptoms when you said you would not, the first step is to admit it to yourself. Once this is done, understand for yourself what it is that you want and, critically, what you need to do to achieve it. Then be clear on both with your manager. Always be honest with yourself and your manager. A little vulnerability – and humility – goes a long way in repairing a relationship that is breaking down. In this instance, it's your move first.

CHAPTER 22
YOUR PEERS

LETTING THEM KNOW

Unlike the formality of the conversation with your manager about Menopause, you're going to have a very different type of conversation with your colleagues and peers. They may have noticed your symptoms in the same way as your manager and are probably equally unaware of its cause unless they've been through it. Just as the interaction will be different, so is the dynamic between you and your peers. You are a group of individuals, each with your own ambitions for your career and long-term prospects. This will drive behaviours that are often underpinned by the organization's culture.

The damaging side effects of competition and positioning are gossip and rumour. This can either be uniformed and naïve or downright malicious. It is vital that you stop this before it becomes an accepted narrative on you and your behaviour. It is incredible how quickly in some organizations story passes into fact.

Every organization is different, and changes over time, too. In each instance, the cohesion of your peers will determine your tactics. If you are part of a tight-knit, mutually supportive group, then collect them together and tell them what is going on and ask for that all-important support to continue. The team cohesion will work to your advantage. It's also likely that when addressing a group, there will be one or more women who have direct experience or men who understand from loved ones, friends or associates.

If your peers are a group in which certain individuals stand apart or are dominant, reducing cohesion, you may wish to take a smaller group or more individual path, and decide who will be formally addressed and who might be comfortable with a more casual approach, dropping it into conversation.

If you have some highly competitive individuals among you, speak to them individually. Of course, there are risks associated with disclosure, albeit these must be measured against the opportunity to neutralize any rumours over which you have no control. That's the key word – neutralize. You need to defuse the tension and spite contained in a rumour. That doesn't mean taking it on, head on, with a directly opposite contention, but carefully and specifically countering it. Evidence clearly always helps. Don't forget, too, that rumours are clearly audible signs; they tell you what people are thinking and saying and give you the opportunity to prove otherwise.

As with your manager, make notes of what was said, when and by whom. Try wherever possible to take them during the meeting or immediately after, to ensure you have as accurate a representation of what was said as possible. You may never need to call on them, but just in case you do, be thorough.

MAINTAINING THE RELATIONSHIP

Once you have had your initial conversation, you will be able to identify those who are empathetic and those who wish to use your situation to their advantage.

For those that are empathetic, make it clear that, in turn, you will support them as and when they need it. Advance notice that you'll help others is in itself a request for help. Mutual backscratching gets bad press, but empathy is a valued commodity and, therefore, one which in its purest form should be utilized.

Most often, personal animosity arises from lack of knowledge or fear of being caught in the Menopause maelstrom on the part of the peer. A calm explanation of what is happening, how you are dealing with it and what to look out for may help.

For those who are overtly seeking to gain an advantage from your situation, step into their space, and ease them to the edge of their moral boundary. Give them every detail of what you are doing to mitigate the unwanted complexities of your situation. While it may seem counterintuitive to 'keep your enemies closer',[38] it will push them to declare whether they have a moral compass. In most situations, self-reflection defuses the problem and normality resumes. You may even create a lasting association from the original tension.

Keep notes, though. Just in case. Indirect victimization is difficult to prove without detailed evidence.

WHAT TO DO IF IT DETERIORATES

You've checked and understand your organization's Menopause policy.

You've taken the 'cultural pulse' of your organization, flagged where there may be hazards and worked out a way around them.

You've taken notes of situations and interactions as they have arisen.

You've been open and honest in communicating your situation and what you're doing about it.

You've asked for support and feedback if you're unaware of the extremes of your behaviour.

You've diffused tension wherever possible through methodical and rational information and explanation.

But you're amid a relentless Menopause, and anything can happen. And that is not taking into account the circumstances of your peers in any regard, which could, for their own reasons, be equally destabilizing. They're not perfect, while you're all over the place.

Your routes back from a deteriorating relationship – or relationships, as it may be with more than just one of your peers – are similar to those with your manager. As with the introductory conversation, you'll need to determine whether it's the group, smaller gatherings or individuals. The simple fact is that for all but the smallest minority, being called out for bad behaviour when someone is at a disadvantage is acutely embarrassing and, if handled politely but resolutely, is usually enough to reset the relationship(s).

Whichever route you take, it is important that you remain dignified throughout. The sad fact is that if you behave in a manner similar to those that are causing you problems, you will be judged more harshly and could validate people's misinformed opinions. Plus, if your symptoms are leading you this way, you could blow a gasket and never recover the situation.

Dignity, dignity, dignity. Never lose it, never let it slip. For everything you're going through, you owe it to yourself.

CHAPTER 23
YOUR TEAM

LETTING THEM KNOW

This is *your* team, the people who work with you on a day-to-day basis, you manage them and recognize that they are individuals who have complex lives, yet they interact and work together to produce amazing things. You may not always be friends, but you're close. You spend a lot of time with these people. They know your wardrobe (at least the work part), your coffee preferences and eating habits. You spend more time with some of them than with your family. Sometimes we (mistakenly) think of them as our family.

They will have noticed you have been behaving differently. Letting them know is more a confirmation than a revelation.

With few exceptions, a group announcement is preferable. Book somewhere that will enable you to discuss this with them privately. I do not mean delving into the nitty gritty of your symptoms, but I do mean that you will need to be vulnerable to show how difficult this is. It will enable them to ask questions. Allow plenty of time for this, to avoid anything being left out. As in all these instances, there will be relief that there is an explanation and that while it's difficult, it's not terminal.

MAINTAINING THE RELATIONSHIP

Your vulnerability should inspire your team to show empathy and support for your situation. They should also be able to quell rumours and create a positive narrative.

You will need to continue this approach and be prepared to allow your team to call you out if your symptoms get out of hand. While you shouldn't allow accusatory finger-pointing, you should find a method between all of you to speak up about unusual or difficult behaviour.

If you get angry, burst into tears or are short-tempered due to exhaustion, aches and pains or simply just because, you will need to show humility and be able to accept that a team member is stepping in almost as a safety valve. Often women are unaware of the escalation in behaviour until it is too late; by doing this, they are naming it with the aim of neutralizing it and ultimately normalizing it.

You are creating a psychologically safe space for you all. It has the potential to strengthen and bond your team beyond any chest-beating team talk.

WHAT TO DO IF IT DETERIORATES

This approach does make management more complex. You are subjugating yourself, showing your vulnerable underbelly. If you then have to deal with poor behaviour of any kind, it can be complex manoeuvring yourself back into the manager/ subordinate roles, to the degree that you will need to find a space that will enable you to be both vulnerable and a manager. It becomes less binary.

If you have team members who themselves become malicious for their own gain, it is again time to discuss the whys and wherefores of the situation with them in private. Remember, keep detailed notes of what was said and agreed to by whom and when. Unlike dealing with your peers, you have a natural advantage in that you are the manager. Yet treating others with respect, even if their motives are questionable, is again a matter of dignity. Never 'pull rank'; always approach the situation with humanity. It will be repaid for both of you.

There is also the need, as we explored with your peers, to evaluate your own behaviour. Your position is undermined if you can't be honest with yourself. This is particularly so if your team has called you out as you requested but you have denied it. Continually appraise yourself. In fact, this is a period of your management career where self-appraisal needs to occur far more regularly than the appraisal of others.

Managing this complex positioning successfully has the potential to make you an impeccable leader. If you already are, then more impeccable still.

CHAPTER 24
TIPS FOR TRICKY SITUATIONS

These suggestions apply for interactions with your manager, colleagues and team as your relationships develop.

OPEN THE NARRATIVE

My overriding tip for all symptoms is to talk about it openly. There is no shame in saying you are Menopausal, even if the recipient of the information is not supportive.

I faced this dilemma some years ago when nobody was talking about Menopause, and I was in the darkest of places. A friend was coaching me; I was isolated and lonely and felt as though I was losing myself. I then had the epiphany that I had two options: I could either sink without trace, or I could start talking about it. Before this, I had had no way to express my ongoing experience in a social situation.

Within moments I was driven to start talking and, to be honest, I haven't stopped. Now I find that most people want to hear more. I carry no shame at all on this subject, even though my elderly mum was horrified that I wanted to discuss Menopause openly. I have never had anyone tell me I was inappropriate or tell me to be quiet. Most appreciated my vulnerability and became more so themselves.

If you are concerned that by admitting that you are in this phase of your life, you will diminish other's opinions of you, stop – that is a construct of our mothers and grandmother's generations. It is there to keep you in your place and isolate you. By opening the narrative on Menopause, you are valuing yourself and validating your experience. This is not about them; it's about you and bringing you in from the cold – or rather hot in this instance.

MAKE VISIBLE LISTS

Lists are great, but it's really easy to forget a list, to close your notepad and with it the memory that you were meant to be doing something.

If you are a list maker, or feel they will be useful, put them in a place that you will definitely see them. We all have places where reminders are particularly effective – perhaps your kitchen unit or the front of your notepad. Wherever it is, it tends to be where there are not already 50 other reminders. Wherever works for you.

TALKING AROUND

If you have lost your verbal recall, when you start a sentence or go to join a conversation names, words or even whole subjects disappear. When this happens, talk around, move on in your own mind to the next point, telling yourself that your brain will deliver up the information when it's ready, or when the stress of forgetting has passed.

As your conversation moves on, your brain often reconnects to the information you were looking for. The dots disperse and rejoin later. It does feel a bit like hide and seek without the excitement. For those who use this tactic, it takes a lot of the stress out of the situation.

I have yet to meet someone who says it works all the time. For the instances when it doesn't, an open declaration often helps. Yes, openness again.

DIARIZE IMMEDIATELY

Smartphones are now ubiquitous. We all have a supercomputer in our pockets. One of your best friends in your phone is the simplest and oldest function: the calendar.

As soon as someone asks you to do something or go somewhere, put it in your phone calendar; that way you have an accurate record. If you don't, there is a chance that by the time you get to your desk or the café you will have forgotten the place, time or even the whole event. Deal with it in the moment; you will thank yourself later. The habit extends beyond this, to dealing with things the moment they arise. Parking something 'for later' risks the idea of 'later' becoming a blacked-out multi-storey for all the things you were supposed to do.

Imagine if you missed the meeting you had set up to discuss your Menopause with your line manager!

GO 'METRO CHIC'

Light colours are out if you suffer from flooding or incontinence. Wearing dark colours buys you time, if only a little. Really, every little bit does help.

If you are teaching, delivering training or any other activity that requires you to stand up in front of others and guide or deliver information, wear clothes that – should the worst happen – allow you to leave the room with your dignity intact.

Have a few handy phrases that will seamlessly direct people to work among themselves while you glide swanlike out of the room and to the nearest toilet. This brings me on to the last point. If you are fairly nomadic for your work, always ask where the nearest Ladies' toilet or restroom is before events occur. Again, every little bit helps.

HOT FLUSH MELTDOWNS

Hot flushes tend to rob you of intelligent thought and cohesive conversation, whether it is because of the stress involved or because your entire sensory system is overloaded. It may be a good idea to make a note of what you were saying, doing or thinking just as you felt the heat start to creep up your torso or prickle your cheeks. This takes some of the stress away and creates a placeholder for you to return to. This isn't seamless, but it helps. And you need to be rational and quick – not always easy.

If you are with a colleague and hot flushes are coming thick and fast, declare what is going on. This will allow the person you are with to understand why you are acting unusually and normalize the situation. Do bear in mind that this may be your colleague's first introduction to the subject if you haven't yet managed to have the conversation. While this chapter assumes all such conversations are planned, sometimes they may just happen as your body temperature soars. Tick it off the list.

CHAPTER 25
YOUR ORGANIZATION

If while managing your own Menopause you have an oppor-tunity – due to your formal role or informal influence – to change the attitude and approach that your organization takes toward Menopause, do not pass it by. You are duty bound.

As we have not historically been open to discussing Menopause, it is not surprising that both women and men are uninformed and ill-prepared to deal with it. The goal is to open the narrative and normalize Menopause.

It should be part of the employee value proposition (EVP), of the onboarding process and of management training and awareness. No one should fear raising the issue, requesting help or adjustment, or feel that they may be judged or prejudiced in any way during this phase of their life. An inclusive workplace means Menopause is included. It's all very well striving for gender balance and promoting and practising flexible working patterns but, if such a significant period of women's lives remains in the shadows, this effort counts for little.

Remember that when a woman's symptoms have subsided, she becomes far more focused and driven than she was before. Women are always an asset to the organization, but these women are becoming powerhouses. The organization doesn't want those powerhouses moving to a more understanding and supportive competitor.

In addition, those women who have been through Menopause are a ready-made source of positive mentoring for those just starting this phase of their life. They should be encouraged and supported in offering this guidance and reassurance.

MENOPAUSE CHAMPIONS

The experience of a bad Menopause has to count – for you and for others. It can't all be for nothing. It is vital that women who have been through it act as champions for those about to, or who are experiencing difficulty.

Most organizational change projects create a team of 'change champions', conduits between leadership and those affected, carriers of information and advocates for the change taking place. Menopause should be no different. It's a change that is less predictable than most corporate change programmes, more difficult and painful (albeit listening to some foot soldiers of the organization you would doubt it) and affects far more people than the new Enterprise Resource Planning (ERP) system.

Most women who stand up and drive change within organizations are those who have had a difficult Menopause. They want to create a support network within the organization, not just to share stories but to ensure the organization recognizes that it needs to support women and help them maintain their careers. This usually works informally on multiple levels, including intranet chat groups and face-to-face gatherings.

Organizations can choose to harness this strength and experience if they wish and turn informal, unplanned and sporadic support into beneficial, planned and freely available assistance and encouragement. Everyone would benefit, not just those within their Menopause.

How improved would all our work relationships be? One day, who knows, you may not even need this book. Who will be first?

CHAPTER 26
SUMMARY

WHAT WE LEARNED

Menopause has long been a topic that both women and men have been uncomfortable openly discussing. It has been confined to the shadows and seen simply as a women's problem. Our workplaces simply reflect our societal prejudices and pressures. However, with the increasing number of women in the workplace across all levels of seniority, there is growing pressure to recognize this phase of a woman's life in the workplace and society as a whole.

The issue for many women is that all of this often occurs just at the point they are about to move to the next level of their career or possibly change their career all together. It also occurs for those who have had children, just as they are back in control of their time and ambitions, as their children start school, secondary school or university.

Our ability to review and assess potential employers via rating sites drives a growing need for employers to demonstrate their 'value proposition' to become an employer of choice. A company's wellbeing policies, management approach and team culture sit at the core of this appeal. Employers who wish to attract the best people, at what is generally the peak of their careers, are starting to recognize the criticality of visibly supporting women through this phase of their lives.

The law under the categories of age, sex and disability recognizes Menopause and protects women against prejudice and/or victimization, while calling for organizations to provide, where appropriate, timely support and adjustments throughout their Menopause. The negative publicity and considerable cost surrounding legal cases brought by women against their employer is very real.

We looked at some of the more common symptoms and what to do if you are struggling with them at work. We are a diverse group and what works for one woman might not work for others, but sometimes just looking at solutions or at least tips from a new perspective not only helps but enables us to gain a little more control when we need it most.

WHAT WE DID

We looked at ways to successfully open the conversation about your Menopause symptoms and behaviours with your manager, your peers and your team, and how to keep the interaction going and keep it positive. For each of these, we looked at how to ask for and receive support, how to maintain relationships throughout Menopause transition and, lastly, what to do if things deteriorate.

We prepared for and documented our conversations, both formal and informal, because while tedious, it is a necessary part of protecting your career and your professional standing, which is why you are doing this in the first place.

HOW THIS HELPS

Gaining empathy and support throughout this phase is essential for you to maintain your work relationships within the organization and enable you to continue to develop your career. Thinking you can just struggle through is potentially damaging from many perspectives, not least of which is your sense of self and your identity as a professional, accomplished woman. Being able to open and maintain the narrative on this will promote you as someone who can have the difficult conversations and gain support, all while retaining your dignity throughout. Whatever your job is, you have worked hard to get to this point, and you deserve support.

We are now able to create and maintain healthy working relationships throughout Menopause and beyond. While everything at work is moving ahead extremely well, we shall now look at our personal relationships.

Part IV

PERSONAL

CHAPTER 27

YOUR PERSONAL RELATIONSHIPS:
INTRODUCTION

At the beginning of my Menopause, when every new symptom drove me further into the depths of despair and my behaviour became more and more unreasonable, I was terrified that I would alienate myself from those I loved and needed the most – my husband and children.

I wanted someone to tell me that it would be OK and that as a family unit we would survive this intact.

Nobody told me.

I could only find desperate stories of women being left or leaving to be on their own. At night when I did sleep, I had torrid dreams about my husband walking out on me, refusing to speak to me, even hiding from me. This cycle of fear, knitted together from other women's tales of woe, devastated my confidence in my relationship and, more importantly, in myself as a partner and a mother. This was a terrible place to be.

My husband, the amazing man that he is, calmed me, held me and reassured me. My children, who were still very young, sat with me so I could breathe them in, hold them and tell them that I loved them. Those moments were still, deep and restorative to all of us, but especially me.

I cannot promise you that your relationship will survive, but I can say that there is every chance that it will.

Talking is where this begins and continues. You will need to bring the conversation to the table, especially with your children if you have them, whether they are young or old. Your partner is not a mind reader. Do not assume that they will understand because they have understood before; your Menopause is unique to you. You are both starting from ground zero, whether your partner is male or female.

Throughout this chapter, you will be using all the work you did in **You Now** and **Future You**. It will create the foundation for much of your thinking in this section. You may tweak it or even amend it, but it is always important to stay true to yourself. Resenting yourself or your partner for your decisions is not constructive for long-term wellbeing, either yours or theirs.

In this chapter, we will cover your relationship with your significant other and how you see the next phase with them in it, recognizing that as you change, so your relationship will need to do the same.

We will discuss desire and desirability, plus the fact that your libido can fall through the floor, along with your natural lubrication. Vaginal dryness is incredibly common, and it needs to be discussed openly and without sniggering or embarrassed coughing. This really is the taboo inside the taboo. We need to get over it.

In the second half of this chapter, we will discuss maintaining your relationship with your children, both toddlers and teenagers. This phase can be challenging for both you and them, so we will look at smoothing out some of the bumps in the road.

It is important to note that this book will not cover your relationship with your parents, siblings, in-laws or friends. There simply aren't enough pages to do them justice. What I would say, though, is that if you can speak to your partner and your children and have developed strategies to support you all as a unit, then speaking to others close to you should be a walk in the park. Of course, there are always exceptions, so use the tips in the following pages to help you through.

What we must not forget is that all your managing of relationships at home is having to be undertaken while dealing with the work-related issues we covered in the previous chapter. We cannot overlook the intermingling of struggles from one to the other and back again. With our work and personal lives increasingly enmeshed, it could well be a work-related matter you bring home that sparks an unpredictable reaction, or a personal matter you take to the office that creates a situation you would rather have avoided.

Neither part of your life exists in a vacuum. Mastering your relationships in one area naturally helps you master them in the other. You must focus equally on both.

CHAPTER 28
CONTEXT: SOCIETY

The last 30 years has seen considerable change in the way we enter into and conduct our personal relationships. It is almost comical to remember that when many of us were young, living together was regarded as 'living in sin'. Obviously, the sin was sex before marriage, which I am sure many couples dabbled in, even with the fear of a child out of wedlock or a 'shotgun' wedding. All of this sounds archaic today. Civil partnerships, made applicable in the UK to heterosexual couples through case law in 2018, are to all legal intents and purposes the same as marriage, without the religious element. It is now commonplace to live together in a 'try before you buy' approach. For some, a formal union holds little allure, choosing to remain 'common law' partners throughout, whether they have children or not. Society is now far more accepting of individual choices.

It was also normal to be living at home right up until the time you married, which tended to be in your 20s, after which time if you still hadn't found someone to 'take you on' – someone's actual words, not mine – you were called a spinster, a derogatory term for singledom that thankfully we have discarded. The mere suggestion that we could be entering into our first, second or even third marriage in our 40s and 50s would have been scandalous to most of our parents.

Socially, we live in a very different world today than the one we grew up in, which is both easy to forget and frustrating in that we want it to be more progressive than it is. Menopause and its array of symptoms is not a modern phenomenon. Women have always had them, depending on length of life, and conversations around it have never been easy.

While the evolutionary dynamics are the same – one person loves another, wants to be with them and wants to be intimate with them – the way in which we hope to conduct ourselves and live with that person has changed, because our role in society has changed. This, added to our modified expectations of support and empathy as we enter Menopause, means that yet again we are carving a path through unchartered territory.

CHANGING EXPECTATIONS

As girls, we were fed a whole heap of nonsense about relationships and how we were expected to behave in them. Think Disney. Many of our parents and grandparents, who were often our only guides to relationship etiquette, were products of the Victorian and post-war childrearing and marriage behavioural codes: head down, have lots of children and don't complain, whatever you do.

Divorce as we know it only came into effect in 1984.[39] The social stigma attached to divorce meant that many couples stayed together when they shouldn't have. I know this because

my parents were one of those couples. My mother was ostracized by some of our neighbours when she filed for divorce.

Our wider social understanding of women in relationships
was neither joyous nor complementary. Women spent their
adult lives pregnant, bringing up children, and condemned to
a life of washing, scrubbing and cooking. It has been argued
by Ha-Joon Chang and others that the domestic washing
machine has created more significant societal change than any
recent technological invention, including even the internet,
freeing women to work and progress careers like no other
device before it, or since.[40]

Conversely, TV and film fed us perfect couples with perfect
homes, perfect children and perfect lives, but if we scratched
the surface, things were not as rosy as they seemed. Women
were disillusioned with their lot but constrained by the social
expectation to be stoic and manage in silence.

Not any longer.

We are still plagued by the desire for a perfect life, more
driven by social media than TV, and women still do most of
the housework.[41] But we are more in control now because
we work, earn our own money and contribute to the household. We have had and continue to have a life outside of
the home. We are affected by external influences, and
make judgments based on our own values, not just those of
our partners.

Today we want support from our partners. If we have children, we want our partners to share the load, we want them to be our very own cheerleader, and we want them to stand by us when Menopause is in full swing. But the social limitations and stereotypes are not that far behind us, which means we need to carve out our own path and define how to pass through this phase successfully, while remaining a bonded and loving couple.

STEREOTYPES

Look back at old Pathé films covering the ideal home exhibition from the 1950s and 60s. Their persistent focus on the woman's place being in the kitchen and subservient to her husband's wishes is depressing. It is no wonder that women aged due to exhaustion combined with boredom brought on by monotonous labour. I can remember the excitement in our house when my mum bought a front-loading washing machine that didn't need monitoring and, in time, when she bought a microwave. Progress was expensive and it moved slowly in our house. The reality is the same in many of our childhoods.

Women were expected to be happy to wait at home for their husbands to return, having polished everything to within an inch of its existence and prepared 'meat and two veg', ready to be served the moment they walked through the door, greeting them with a gin and tonic or, failing that, a good strong cup of sweet tea, in hand. Following this line of thinking, sex was something that men expected, and women delivered. I appreciate that for many couples, sex was then as it is now a precious and intense connectedness that cements the relationship.

While the limitations and predictability of women's worlds might have been reassuring during their early years of marriage, by the time they were into their third decade of it, for many it must have felt like a prison.

When we look back at images of women, even in the last century, they are either youthful, beautiful, petite and pert, ultimately biddable, or they are matronly, hair in rollers, head scarf on and permanently in an apron. Women went from naïve or vixen-like to undesirable, sexless and bitter. It is time to question the stereotypes on a deeper level.

After decades of childbirth, women's vaginas and vulvas must have been ravaged. Pain during sex must have been common. Vaginal atrophy and dryness, while difficult to discuss now, must have been beyond most women, their partners and GPs. Help must have felt like an impossibility. Incontinence must have been rife. Add to this the social stigma surrounding anxiety, depression and panic attacks. I am sure that more than one woman was sectioned during this phase of her life. It's difficult to know, as families hid this type of illness for fear of social exclusion. The Victorian image of a lunatic asylum and its inmates still hangs over our subconscious even today, let alone 50 years ago.

Many names have been sewn into our social subconscious that we wouldn't think of using, yet still they linger: 'crone', often preceded by 'dried up', 'old' or 'haggard', 'dried up old prune' or 'typical mad woman'. We even had a derogatory and unattractive name for osteoporosis, 'dowager's hump'. Of course, you can suffer from osteoporosis whether you are married or widowed or, for that matter, rich or poor.

If these stereotypes, and this type of name calling occurred within our lifetimes, both us and our partners, no matter how hard we try, will be haunted by them when times are tough. Do they inspire you as a partner to stick around? Unlikely. Do they make you, as a woman, feel sexy and empowered? Even less likely. They undermine your ability to maintain your relationship on an equal footing.

Many of our negative and demeaning stereotypes for women in their mid-40s to mid-60s are based on misunderstandings due to zero ability to talk about and normalize Menopausal symptoms in an empathetic way. The only way to ensure they end is to reverse the trend.

Let's put a stake in the ground now and start the conversation.

CHAPTER 29
CONTEXT: PRIVATE LIVES

Our significant relationship with the person we call our partner, husband or wife holds a pivotal place in our lives. They are the person we lean on, turn to and rely on. They are the one who holds our fragile heart, and they know our dark and lighter side, which is why it is so important to us that they hold the relationship space for both of us while we are less able.

COMPLEX LIVES

'You never really know what happens behind closed doors' was a phrase often said when I was a child. Usually with pursed lips and in a hushed and slightly suspicious tone. If I look back now, life seemed so infinitely simple. What is the same, though, is that you can never be certain how complicated a person's life is on the inside, and certainly not from the outside looking in with judgment or preconceived perceptions. And because of societal changes, we have far more complicated private lives than our parents would have dreamed of.

Many of us have a career, which means we work long hours – probably longer than our fathers did, when jobs were for life and many employees worked a nine to five ticket – and carry the associated stress of this with us. This does mean we earn our own money, have independence and, above all, have choice. It is increasingly common to find women as the principle earner in the household, with all the pressure that that brings.

Women can choose whether or not to have children (fertility and biology dependent). If they do, they can have one or multiple families depending on their relationship history.

Add to this mix stepchildren and ex-partners, and suddenly our home life becomes incredibly complicated, at times politicized and often chaotic.

That is not to say that it can't be fantastic. It most certainly can. But to make our complex lives work, especially with the added pressure of Menopause, there is an increased level of commitment needed from all parents and children. Without it, it can so easily become toxic, causing bitterness and resentment.

The other modern phenomena is 'boomerang kids'. Just as you were getting used to having either one less mouth to feed or more privacy to reinvigorate your sex life, you find that your strapping 21-year old returns from university on heat, with considerable debt, unpleasant habits and a desire to eat constantly. The level of debt young people have to manage on their return from university, combined with an ever-increasing cost of housing, means that many can't afford to move out. Yet for some, the idea of living in a shared house or bedsit is unpalatable, especially when home is so comfortable. While not a completely new phenomenon, it is becoming socially acceptable to move back home after leaving university.

There are our parents, as well. We are a 'sandwich generation'. Because we are all living longer, we need to care for and support our parents through the last decades of their lives. This can be emotionally, physically and financially draining.

All these complexities make up our modern lives. We are emotionally pulled from one to the next, which can leave little time for our partners and the glue that bonds us together. You will need to change this; success at this time requires investment of a nonfinancial type from both you and your partner.

EXPECTATION MANAGEMENT

You are changing in a way that you have not experienced since puberty. The chemicals you know as hormones, which cyclically surged around your system every month, are making their curtain call before settling in their steady state. As Christiane Northrup says in her book, *The Wisdom of Menopause*,[42] "hormone levels after Menopause are identical to those in girls before puberty," and that our hormones influence our behaviours ensuring "we compromise" and "maintain the balance and peace." She also notes that we are "extraordinary caretakers" during our reproductive years. While we don't lose our ability to care or nurture, or to maintain the peace, we do have an innate drive to be more of ourselves and far more determined to stand up for what is important to us. We are becoming focused on our own self and our ambitions, as discussed in **You Now**.

Because of all these things, those you love will need to change the way they interact with you as will you with them.

If you are having a difficult time of it, your partner and your children will be trying to manage your fluctuating moods on a day-by-day, minute-to-minute basis. This is exhausting and stressful for all involved. Let's not deceive ourselves – you can be very difficult to be with.

The combustible mix of symptoms and changes in your perspective and approach to life can herald a difficult period in your relationships. Of course, this can simply be because those around you are not aware of what's going on. Everyone has expectations based on experience; your partner and children are no different. They have an expectation of how you will be, based on the 'you' of before. They are having to adapt to the new you as it appears, which can remove a level of expected stability. Being decent and kind to each other is critical. There may be a bit of shouting along the way but remembering what is important and precious in your relationships will anchor you throughout the storm.

Communication is king, queen, prince and princess when trying to maintain any relationship, but it is especially so when it is about maintaining a bond that is under pressure from previously unforeseen symptoms. Get this right, and you, your partner and your children will find this experience considerably less stressful. Remember, they are probably wondering where the woman they used to know has gone, and who this stranger is that's taken her place? They are indirectly experiencing your Menopause, with even less understanding than you have. A large part of this chapter is about helping you prepare for and have productive conversations with those you love. The aim of the conversations is to maintain the closeness between you and develop empathetic strategies to support you and the family unit throughout.

THE GRASS IS ALWAYS GREENER

Same-sex and heterosexual couples can suffer from the same pressures at this time, in that one party can have no understanding of the other's experience. However, what is unique to same-sex couples is the potential dynamic of two Menopausal women in the same household.

Having said this, men in heterosexual couples undergo a reassessment of their own lives. This is commonly and derisorily called a 'midlife crisis', commonly associated with the purchase of a fast car or motorbike. At this point, the stereotypical struggling male is often showered with sympathy or a cheeky, knowing smile. "Well, it's a phase, let him do his thing, he'll calm down again." The 'crisis' is deemed natural, almost hormonal, as the downtrodden male seeks to reassert his virility and masculinity.

Empathy must flow both ways in any relationship, especially at this point in life. The caveat here is that it does not give either of you carte blanche to behave abominably, disrespectfully or in any way untrustworthily. There is no excuse for behaving like an arse.

It is all too easy at this time to look outside of the relationship for sex, comfort or simply a sense of normality. This can be either party but, in my experience, it is usually the one who is not experiencing Menopause. Many women have spoken to me about their partners leaving them for Julie in accounts (of course, it's not always Julie, but you get the picture).

If it is you, the Menopausal woman, who is peeking over the fence, be sure this is not your hormones talking, before you make any impulsive decisions. Short-term lust has devastated more than one relationship, and it has also driven many a perpetrator into numerous subsequent poor decisions.

Be sure of your motives before you start down this route.

CHAPTER 30
YOU AND YOUR PARTNER

When you are in an under-resourced state, as women often are during this phase of their lives, it is easy to be drawn into the belief that Menopause is the death knell for your significant relationship. We often hear stories of relationships crumbling under the pressure of symptoms, or women seemingly deciding overnight to leave their partners. Because I knew that I was putting my husband and children under considerable pressure, I focused on ways to prevent that from happening.

When reflecting logically, we know that these stories of relationship breakdowns were probably last-straw situations. That is, there were likely to have been issues, perhaps recognized, perhaps not, in these women's relationships back when the word 'Menopause' meant nothing to either of them.

Menopause does not mean the end of your relationship with your partner, but – and it's a very big but – do not deceive yourself, it can have a profound impact on it.

Before you close the book in fear of what you might read, don't! Many relationships survive this, becoming stronger because of the experience. You and your partner will need to face the changes in whatever way they present themselves and decide how best to manage them between you. But, and this is an equally big but, you will both need to be adults. You will need to respect each other and, very importantly, be prepared to be humble. Recognize when you have behaved unfairly or unjustly, be prepared to build bridges between you and, above everything else, keep communicating. Never. Stop. Talking.

LOVE AND INTIMACY

It is universally recognized that desire and desirability are seriously affected by Menopause. Our sense of both have a vice-like grip on our ability to even contemplate intimacy, let alone sex.

This part of women is complex and linked to many aspects of life, including how they feel about themselves as well as their partner and their relationship. It is common for women to experience marked changes in sexual response and desire during Menopause. Because of this, it can put considerable pressure on intimate relationships. It is important to note that this is the same no matter the gender of the person you choose to share your life with.

As you progress through Menopause, the unexplainable oscillation – between a desperate all-consuming desire to a numb coldness or repulsion, wanting never to be touched again – is confusing for both parties. The questioning of your own desirability or confidence in your body, which may have changed for many reasons including illness, is corrosive to your sexual self.

There are a vast array of influencers and disrupters at play here. Some you can take immediate control of. For others, it's not so easy.

INFLUENCERS

Unsurprisingly, your hormones are having a huge influence on your sense of desire. There are three at play here: oestrogen and progesterone, which we all know about as they were discussed in Chapter 4, and testosterone, which we usually think of as a male hormone. Testosterone is present in women's bodies and its decline can seriously affect our sex drive. If a lack of it is the problem, you will need to see a Menopause specialist,[43] as most GPs will not prescribe it.

The effect that the drop in hormones has on your body and your psychology has a direct influence on your sense of being a desirable woman and, in turn, being prepared to let your own desire bubble to the surface.

An example of this is body image. How you feel about your body defines your readiness to let someone else experience your body. Many women watch their weight and feel sexier when they are in control of it. Getting your favourite outfit out and finding that there is a two-inch gap between either side of the zip often has a detrimental effect on your sense of desirability. As is putting on new underwear, only to find your bra strap creates its own figure eight on your ever-spreading back and underarm fat, and the knickers are like cheese wire around your hips.

There is a biological reason for this. The reducing oestrogen production in your ovaries means your body seeks to create it from other sources. Your fat produces oestrogen, and the fat around your middle is particularly (and annoyingly) good at it. This means your body starts to store fat in this area in order to produce the hormone it needs. What you see from the outside is a sudden and seemingly inexplicable weight gain, and the appearance of belly fat. This, combined with a drop in your metabolic rate as you have got older, means it is even harder to lose the weight you are putting on.

It will take more than saying 'no' to the mid-morning custard creams to shift it. This is a biological response. However, comfort eating is not, and women often feel driven to this due to a range of symptoms including sleep deprivation (insomnia and night sweats), fatigue, depression and anxiety. Diminished self-confidence can have women reaching for a comfort croissant which, conversely, does them no favours. It drives their confidence further into the negative.

When a woman suffers from insomnia or night sweats, the sheer exhaustion of sleep deprivation affects women's desire for their partners. Women report that they feel so tired that the only mood they are prepared to get into is the one that enables them to experience sustained and fitful sleep. Not tonight, darling.

DISRUPTERS

Menopause goes right to the heart of a relationship's physicality. Its symptoms affect women's sense of desire or desirability. It also makes it tricky when starting out with a new relationship. You will need to go slower in many ways, so that you, your body and your partner can enjoy intimacy during this period of transition and beyond.

Around 58% of post-Menopausal women experience vaginal dryness.[44] It's likely the figure is much higher, as many women feel too embarrassed to discuss this even with their GP. The first sign that this is happening is reduced natural lubrication during sex. Of course, if there is no foreplay, no hugging, kissing or touching to get you started, then this will be part of the issue. For most women who are suffering from dryness, no amount of touching or rubbing or anything else around the vulva (lips) and clitoris helps. In fact, it usually only makes things sorer.

The drop in oestrogen is at fault here. This causes the skin and tissue to become thinner and less elastic, which means that it is damaged more easily during foreplay and sex. This causes pain, tearing and, in some cases, bleeding. It is important to note that any unexpected bleeding during or after sex should be checked by a GP to ensure that it is not a symptom of something more sinister.

Vaginal dryness can be experienced in degrees from a little discomfort during sex to constant and severe pain that affects your ability to live a normal life. The tissue becomes so fragile that any form of friction is excruciating. Those cheese wire knickers won't help.

Yet help is at hand; your first port of call is specialist moisturizers and lubrication. Use one that is natural and won't upset your delicate pH balance or skin. Do not use the mass-produced brands you see everywhere. They will irritate your skin and dry it out further. If you are unsure which to choose, ask your GP.

If you need additional assistance, then your GP should be able to help. Vaginal (local) oestrogen in the form of gels or tablets (inserted into the vagina using an applicator) are a very effective treatment. They are an extremely low dose, which only reaches the tissue of the vagina and doesn't pass around the body. Therefore, it does not carry the same concerns as HRT.

This leads us on to an increased susceptibility to thrush and bacterial vaginosis, causing unusual and smelly discharge. This is because the drop in oestrogen affects the pH balance inside your vagina. Vaginal oestrogen will resolve this, as it will for repeated UTIs (Urinary Tract Infections), which women are also prone to at this time.

Leakage or incontinence is also an issue for many women. We discussed this symptom in **You Now**. Vaginal or local oestrogen can benefit here, too, as it helps the tissue regain some of its elasticity. And don't forget your pelvic floor exercises. These have an added benefit of improving the sexual experience for you and your partner.

Hot flushes too can impact your feeling of desirability. It can be difficult to feel anything other than uncomfortable when you feel as slippery as a bar of wet soap the moment the two of you become in any way intimate. You will be so hot you will not be able to stand your partner's body heat next to you. Hot flushes are indiscriminate; they will occur at the most inconvenient times.

Meanwhile, the embarrassment and unpredictability of flooding can be highly disruptive to women's sex lives. Your GP should be able to offer you options to help you manage this symptom.

All the above symptoms can be highly disruptive to your sense of desirability and terminal to your libido. You will need to address these issues as an adult. It can feel excruciatingly embarrassing to talk about these things, yet a short conversation with your GP should result in a prescription that should help, if not resolve, the issue. If you choose not to, these symptoms can and likely will seriously affect your sex life and, in turn, your relationship. If the relationship is new, the increased vulnerability you will feel will manifest itself in other ways too. They will not go away on their own; they need to be addressed to have any hope of being resolved.

There is absolutely no need to suffer in silence. Intimacy is an important part of any new relationship; it should be enjoyable and exciting. To ensure this is the case, seek support now.

For all symptoms, communication very importantly opens the door for your partner to support you with some level of empathy. We are not taught how to have conversations about how our intimate bodily functions are affecting the connection between us and another. It can be excruciatingly awkward, yes, but this one area alone can devastate a relationship if it is not addressed reasonably early.

The next step is for you to go and seek help. This is important on many levels, not least because it's about you taking back control. There are many options out there; some you will have to work hard to access, be prepared to fight for, or decide if you can afford to pay for medical assistance. However, the act of seeking help gives you the opportunity to draw a breath possibly for the first time in a long time.

BEING ON HEAT

This is at the other end of the scale and is common during peri-Menopause. Many women confess to a massively increased sex drive, desperately wanting to jump on top of any suitable or not-so-suitable mate. They are happy to punch below their weight. This is often irrespective of whether they are in a stable and loving relationship or not. It would seem that the body is literally having its last hurrah with its remaining eggs.

This can be very disconcerting for those in a stable loving relationship. It can also be embarrassing at the office Christmas party.

THE ART OF A SUCCESSFUL 'M' CONVERSATION WITH YOUR PARTNER

Unlike the workplace conversations, this really is your responsibility. You are the one who is going to have to raise this, and you are the one who needs to continue the conversation as and when the need arises. Your partner is unlikely to understand what has caused the changes in you, whether they be physical, emotional, psychological or behavioural. In addition to this, the mass of symptoms you are experiencing are often iceberg-like to the person on the outside looking in. They really don't know the enormity of how you are feeling unless you tell them. They are not mind readers.

Choose a time when you know you won't be interrupted, whether that be by work, children, friends or your favourite TV programme. Next, try to ensure that the environment is calm. Seclusion is not always possible at home, so a private nook in a café or a walk in the park might be better. It's your call. Remember that you are about to be humble and vulnerable; you need to feel safe and wherever you choose needs to feel private.

Prepare what you are going to say. Use the table in the first chapter where you identified your symptoms and the interdependency work you did in **You Now**. Think in detail about what it is like for you, what happens and when. Be prepared to listen to what it is like for them. It is likely that you may need to reference the chronology of your core symptom as well. This breadth of information will enable them to understand the complexity and depth of your experience.

The first part of your conversation is education. You are supporting their learning so that they can help you through the ups and downs. Even if they have experienced a previous partner's Menopause or even their own, while it might be similar, it won't be the same.

GETTING OR ASKING FOR SUPPORT

There are two parts to this. First, most people want to support their partners. It is, therefore, important to graciously take the help they offer. Some of us, for a multitude of reasons, find it very difficult to accept help from others. If this is you, it's important to remember that help given at this time can make a considerable difference in the quality of your life and maintain the connection with your partner.

By refusing help or begrudgingly taking it, it creates a divide between you and the giver. Sadly, the resulting divide is often filled with resentment and cynicism from both parties. It effectively isolates you and excludes you from an important part of bonding with your partner. It can create an unhealthy precedent for the future.

The second part of this is that if help is not offered for whatever reason, blatantly ask for it. You are in a relationship with this person, you are a team of two, and it is completely acceptable to ask for support and to keep asking for it when you need it. If this is new for either of you, better late than never, because Menopause is a completely unique experience, and one that drives change on many levels.

KEEP IT SIMPLE

When thinking about what you are going to say, remember to be clear about which symptoms you are experiencing and their impact. Be factual. This should be relatively straightforward as you will have established this already in **You Now**.

I suggest initially talking around what Menopause is in general, and then what it is for you specifically. If you are having extreme symptoms, it is likely that your partner will be relieved that there is a normal explanation for the changes in you.

Next, be clear with yourself about what you want from this conversation, and the help you want from your partner. Make it achievable. By this I mean they shouldn't have to become Mother Teresa, James Bond and Sigmund Freud rolled into one in order to support you on a day-to-day basis. It might be a step too far. Think about simple things they can incorporate into their day, which is more than likely packed already.

Test it out on yourself. If you were asked to do what you're asking them to do, could you and/or would you do it? If the answer is no, then is it reasonable to ask it of them? Alternatively, if the answer is yes but at a stretch, can you amend it to make it easier? Be clear that it is something that you will be asking for only on occasion and in extreme conditions. If this is the case, then make sure it's a reality. If you tell your partner that you will only call on them in this way under extreme circumstances, yet those circumstances seem to occur every day, then you will need to readdress this. It's a bit like Aesop's[45] little boy who always cried wolf.

Think it through, be honourable and keep it simple.

MAINTAINING YOUR RELATIONSHIP

Now that you have declared that you are Menopausal and explained the symptoms that you are suffering from, work together to create some strategies to manage them.

Telling someone to calm down just as the needle is about to hit the red zone is usually inadvisable. They don't have the resources in that moment to recognize that they are behaving in a way that they might regret later. Likewise, telling someone who is depressed or suffering from anxiety to cheer up and look at the bright side of things is usually going to have the opposite effect. Therefore, while you are talking, think about ways that this can be broached without you going intergalactic.

Next, how do you usually manage issues or problems that arise? Do you talk things through, seek consensus or, at the very least, come to an agreed-upon plan of action? Alternatively, do you fight it out until one person dominates the other into submission, whether that be through arguing, passive aggression or silence? If it's any of the latter, now is not the time and, in fact, I am not sure when it will be the time. One thing is for certain: they are not conducive to a positive, flexible and supportive outcome and do not bode well for the future.

Humility is not only important, it is also very endearing. If you have been a fire-breathing monster over the last few months, or as mad as a box of frogs, admit it. The person you are being is not the person that you are. You are in transition.

MAINTAINING THE CONVERSATION

It is important to keep talking to your partner, as they are unlikely to be aware of the nuances of your Menopausal experience. Conversations of this type are not one-hit wonders. You shouldn't feel relief that it's over and done with. You will need to keep returning to it, not least because the severity of your symptoms will fluctuate as you move through your Menopause. It is possible that you will gain some symptoms while losing others. If there are no outward signs that this is the case, there is no way your partner will be able to guess this.

These conversations are obviously far more emotional and far less rigid than work conversations. Be prepared for some home truths regarding how difficult you can be. If this is the case, face it; denying it shows disregard for your partner and the bond between you. You are also deceiving yourself and withholding an opportunity for you to take control. This is not a case of 'if I can't see it, it doesn't exist.' If you don't like those parts of you and would rather ignore them, good luck. They won't go away so easily and will only continue to upset you and your partner until you recognize them and act. That decisive moment passes the control to you.

Lastly, you will not only have your symptoms to deal with, but underneath that you will be changing as discussed in **You Now** and **Future You**. While the prospect of this is exciting, you will need to communicate how this impacts you both as a unit.

ACTIVE LISTENING

Active listening is a concept that all coaches, counsellors and psychotherapists learn very early on in their training. It doesn't take enormous intellect or time to learn, but its effect is profound. People respond to being listened to. They feel heard and understood. The concept simply means you are listening with your whole self, focused completely on what the other person is saying and how they are saying it.

We are all guilty of being in a conversation with one person while thinking about someone or something else. Unfortunately, many people continuously listen like this. Frequently, the person talking knows that this is the case, even if it's at a subliminal level.

We have all seen TV programmes where one person is talking to their partner, friend or family member who is reading the paper and their distracted "yes dear" or "mmm" entered at the critical points in the conversation are completely unsatisfactory to the person speaking. They are not really listening; they are simply propping up the talker. Conversations of this nature are not going to support you as a couple during this phase of life.

Remember, this is an end and a beginning and, as such, you need to reconnect with each other and establish the new rules of engagement.

Ask your partner to sit with you, to clear their mind and listen. It can be exhausting listening like this, especially if you or your partner are not used to it. Start with small conversations and work your way up.

If you are both competing for airtime, this is not listening. You are occupying your brain, constructing your own thoughts, points of argument or killer questions. Agree between yourselves that you each get a certain amount of time to talk, then there are questions. Use an object that is held only by the speaker – if you're not holding it, you can't speak. It focuses us on how much we actually interrupt or drift. This may initially seem too formal, but it can be a necessity while you learn how to listen actively.

WHAT TO DO IF IT DETERIORATES

The process of sitting down to discuss the changes in your behaviour, emotions or priorities is not an opportunity for either of you to offload previous or unrelated points of disagreement. This is about your Menopause and not the fact that one of you doesn't put the lid on the toothpaste or leaves dirty cups all over the place. If everything merges into an argument, no matter how trivial, it's not going to go well.

All couples argue from time to time. It is perfectly normal. Some couples, though, take arguing to a new level. It could be a sign that the relationship is struggling, or that they haven't learned another way to resolve issues as yet, and for some it's part of who they are.

Whichever best describes you as a couple, it is likely that you have a well-worn argument routine. Person A says something that drives person B crazy, so they respond in a certain way, which drives person A crazy, so they respond, and so on and so on. There is some security in this process. We know the steps, even if it's subconscious and it protects us from facing fears or truths and drives us into predictable power or victim positions. You don't need me to tell you that this is not healthy. Support does not come from dominance or criticism, but from empathy, understanding and equality.

If words such as '... and another thing ...' or '... typical ...' are said at any point or if there is angry finger-pointing, you are now entrenched in arguments rather than constructive conversations. This takes some effort to fix and is exhausting for both of you.

Gary Chapman, in his book *The 5 Love Languages*,[46] talks about how successful couples learn how to build bridges between them during arguments. This can be done in a multitude of ways, whether it's one person telling a joke, making a funny quip or perhaps a reference to an earlier happier time. One couple I spoke to make a cup of tea or coffee for the other and put eight or nine spoonfuls of sugar in it, when neither of them takes sugar. As a nonconfrontational sign that they had got out of hand, it worked for them every time. Building successful bridges requires both of you to be prepared to cast a line and catch it. It may take a few goes, but successful couples know that these actions require commitment.

SEPARATION AND DIVORCE

It would be naïve to think that all couples survive this phase of life. There are a multitude of reasons why they don't and it's not just Menopause. The accusation "you're not the woman I married" is indeed true. After Menopause, you will have changed. Your own re-evaluation of life could lead you to decide that you are both moving in different directions.

The heterosexual divorce rates for England and Wales[47] show in general a downward trend in divorce across all age groups until you get to age 50. Divorce for women over the age of 50 is seeing an upward trend. Marriage and divorce among same-sex couples has not been legal for long enough to provide any form of trend data.

If you find yourself in this position, be clear as to why and what you hope your life will be at the other end. Return to **You Now** and **Future You** and be clear and honest with yourself. Divorce is often complex and filled with vitriol and bitterness. You will not be the same at the end of it. Focus on what your future holds, and it will help to draw you through those times when you question yourself.

If you find that your partner is the one who has declared that this is the end, allow yourself to mourn for what might have been if you need to. It is then vital to focus on your outcome. Because now you are at the centre of your future.

If you have children, they are your priority, especially if they are young or going through puberty. Protecting them from the depths and the deterioration of your relationship and potentially poor behaviour is vital. Metaphorically slugging it out in front of them does not help them or their growing understanding of what relationships are and how they work.

Lastly, be aware of your rights and, very importantly, the money that you both have. Again, if you have children, ensure that their future welfare is protected.

CHAPTER 31
FOR YOUR PARTNER

◆

Dear partner, this is for you.

Menopause can be a big deal, and maybe your partner is having a hard-enough time to have given you this book. This is unlikely to be easy. Sorry. This is not a slight blip in the road; you are effectively on a journey together that will take some time to get to the end – estimates range from 4 to 14 years. There will be challenges and setbacks but, at the end of it, you and your partner have the potential to be astounding. But you will both need to work together and have a clear understanding of what you want from this second phase of your lives together.

The fact that she has given you this book is an indication that she loves you and wants your support. She is also saying that she is in need of some words to successfully communicate with you what this is like.

THE ICEBERG EFFECT

Menopause is like an iceberg, in that the majority of what is going on is beneath the surface. You might think you are getting the rough end of the deal. While I sympathize with you, I can assure you, you are not.

Your partner's hormones are slowly but surely receding to their steady post-Menopausal state. They play such a pivotal role in her sense of who she is, and how she is in the world that as they diminish, they cause havoc with her sense of self and her day-to-day behaviour. Their increasing absence delivers a whole host of symptoms as well.

You are likely at the sharp end of her symptoms, vicariously experiencing them with her. Most women require reassurance that their partners are still committed to them and the relationship. It's easy to believe that you're all right and that this is her problem. To some degree it is, but it would be unfair of you to believe that this was completely the case.

You are a team of two that no doubt has had to face adversity before. How did you manage it? What was the dynamic between you? Is this the same or different? If it's the same, due to its unpredictability or that one of you needs additional consideration and support, you already have a model of how to work together. If it's different, what kind of different is it? If it's different because it was you who needed support and now it's her, then there is an element of *quid pro quo*. How did she manage it, what did she do that was so effective and also, what was ineffective and why? These are all things you both can learn from.

Discuss between you what worked and what didn't and identify what you can use here.

WHAT IS THIS THING THAT'S
HAPPENING TO HER ... AND ME?

Earlier in this book, you will find a section on symptoms where we discuss the variability in women's experience of Menopause by duration, type and their severity. Please read through it, as awareness is a considerable part of successfully supporting your partner.

First, Menopause is not a sprint, which is essentially what the monthly period experience was, or even an 800m run, which was pregnancy. No, Menopause is an endurance race, and it goes on for years. With this in mind, it's important to make yourself aware of what your partner might be experiencing and think about what support she might need.

Please note, this does not give her a licence to be revolting to you without any form of comeback. If her behaviour makes her more difficult to handle than a bag of poisonous snakes, you have a right to say so. This is about creating a psychologically safe place for both of you to air your grievances without a shouting match or sulky silences. This space should be non-judgmental, with no fear of consequences. You are adults and now is the time to behave like it.

FIRESIDE CHAT

Where do the two of you get uninterrupted time to chat face-to-face? Whether over breakfast, dinner or some other time, whenever it is, choose a day when you know neither of you will be preoccupied or focused on something else. Be clear that this is a conversation about understanding what is happening and what it feels like for her. Make sure you are actively listening – a method of intently listening to what the other person is saying whilst giving them your full attention. If you need any pointers in how to do this, there is a whole section on it in Chapter 30.

Once you have actively listened, ask questions and share how you feel about it. Please note, this about listening, sharing and reconnecting, not about point scoring or arguing. If you find that you are descending into this, you may need to walk away and come back later. You are both adults and equal partners – you are not a winner or a loser, a leader or a follower, in charge or subservient. You are a team of two equal parts.

BEING A CHEATING W*NKER

Let's not be coy here. Frankly, it's insulting. If you are or considering having an affair because your partner no longer looks as good as she used to, or as good as Julie in accounts, or because her symptoms make her difficult to be with, or at least not as easy or as pliable as she used to be, or lastly because her sex drive is not what it was or sex is a whole lot more complex than it used to be with lubes, soreness and a general lack of expected responsiveness – get over yourself. None of these are a reason for an affair. That's a cowardly way out.

Instead, they are a reason to talk about how you feel as an adult. Perhaps you need to face the fact that you and she are ageing;

maybe you are struggling with that. You might have a need to feel virile, potent, sexual, and that you need to feel like you are retaining some of your youthful charms. You may even feel as though this experience is seemingly robbing you of that. It really is time to talk.

While the sexual side of your relationship may have suffered for a multitude of reasons, I would challenge you to question whether you are party to that reason. Women need gentler handling and the recognition that they are a whole person during this phase of their life. By this I mean that being resentful or oblique in other areas of your life together will impact her sense of desire for you, as well as her sense of desirability. As Dr Ruth[48] says, foreplay for women starts with the postcoital cuddle after the last time you had sex. Essentially, sex is not simply an isolated event.

If you have strayed or are on the verge, be clear with yourself as to why. Stepping off this cliff can be terminal to your relationship. If you think things are difficult now, it bears no relation to how difficult it will be to repair what could be easily broken.

DOUBLE STANDARDS

I am frequently staggered at people's beliefs that they have the right to criticize women at this time in their lives. It's difficult enough managing insomnia, depression, weight gain, vaginal dryness, hot flushes, flooding, itchy skin and achy joints – to name but a few symptoms – without an overweight, beer-drinking lout shouting that "You've let yourself go, haven't you love?"

There is so much wrong with statements such as this, that I and most women could write a thesis-length paper on this alone. I will, however, say only this; judge yourself before you even think of judging others.

And – breathe.

PLANNING TOGETHER

When going through some periods of intense change, it is natural to resist extending yourself too far or worry you won't be able to cope with any additional modifications to your routine.

As previously stated, during Menopause you are facing a level of unprecedented change, all of which is outside of your immediate control. Just as with symptoms in **You Now**, you can control what you do next, and both of you can control what you do as a couple. This is where you reach the pivotal point and where the fun begins.

Instead of withdrawing to base camp to check the contents of your rucksack, only to look up at the summit wistfully sometime in the future, push on.

Turn up the level of change and ambition. Focus on those things you do have control over. Just as before, if you turn your focus outward instead of inward and look to the future, it will draw you forward and, in doing so, give both of you a sense of control and empowerment that may have felt sorely lacking.

What is critical here is to do it together. Running roughshod over your partner and their ambitions is not productive. This seems obvious, but many in their attempt to gain control, literally control everything. You are in a partnership; find a method where you share the adventures between you. Maybe take turns or divide the year and/or budget. Whichever way you work it, make sure you are both heard and, very importantly, both fulfilled.

Fill in the table below with your partner. These are the same set of questions she answered for her five-year plan, simply from a 'we' perspective. You go first. That way you will both understand your own ambitions before you look to find common ground.

Vision	Your perspective	Your partner's perspective
For the next five years to go just the way we'd like, it will be like what?	A	…
When it's like [A] is there anything else about [A]?	…	…
For it to be like that, we'll be like what?	…	…
What will we see/hear when it's like [A]?	…	…
How will we know it's like [A]?	…	…

Where	Your perspective	Your partner's perspective
In five years' time, where do we want to be?	... **B**	...
When we are [**B**] is there anything else about [**B**]?	...	...
For it to be like that, we'll be like what?	...	...
What will we see/hear when we are [**B**]?	...	...
How will we know we are [**B**]?	...	...
What		
In five years' time, what do we want to be doing?	... **C**	...
When we are [**C**] is there anything else about [**C**]?	...	...
For it to be like that, we'll be like what?	...	...
What will we see/hear when we are [**C**]?	...	...
How will we know we are [**C**]?	...	...

CHAPTER 32
CHILDREN

Our children are incredibly precious, whether they are biologically ours, stepchildren, adopted or fostered. Our love for them runs through every molecule of our bodies. Without a doubt, being a parent is one of the most challenging yet amazing experiences we will ever have. And because of this, the mere suggestion that we could behave in any way that would upset them fills many of us with guilt and pain and adds anxiety to what you are experiencing already. This seemingly provides even more reasons to admit to that nagging feeling that you are a bad mother. It is a lose-lose situation.

Menopause will challenge every behaviour you previously exhibited with your children, especially during those times of stress. Like getting them into and out of bed, breakfast, school, homework, exams, dawning and rampant sexuality, boyfriends, girlfriends, eating, driving, going out late, going to university. This is just a small section of a very long list that changes as your children grow up.

Clearly, your children will experience your Menopause with you. They are quite frequently at the bottom of the list as far as understanding is concerned. They have little or no precedent to fathom why mummy or mum is suddenly no longer the patient, even-tempered, fun-loving and energetic person she once was.

One caveat here: I have spoken to some women who have children in their late teens and early 20s, who were the first to spot the signs. If this is you, hug your children and thank them and the person who told them what Menopausal symptoms are and how they might affect women.

Let's be absolutely honest here: parenting is hard. In fact, it's harder than anything you have done professionally and no one, rather unreasonably, gave you a handbook or offered a three-day intensive training course. You are effectively learning on the job all the time. Work-based imposter syndrome has nothing on this.

It is essential that you speak to your children. You know what works best and how to say it. Prepare yourself; this can feel like the most vulnerable of all the 'M' conversations because you are admitting that your behaviour is causing them difficulties.

In the longer term, you are opening up a narrative for them when they are older. Even if your children are boys, they will have a partner, colleague or friend who will experience Menopause, and it will enable them to support them intelligently and empathetically through it.

I have split this section into younger and older children because the conversations will be different.

SUCCESSFUL 'M' CONVERSATIONS
WITH YOUNGER CHILDREN

First, I think it's important to deal with the myth that all Menopausal women are managing 'empty-nest' syndrome. This is simply not the case. Increasing numbers of women are delaying having children until their late 30s, early 40s, or having children in second or third marriages or relationships. Therefore, it is basic maths that a growing percentage of the female population will be managing Menopausal symptoms while looking after young children.

Young children will simply not understand why mummy has suddenly changed from being loving and caring virtually all the time to being a shouty, grumpy, tearful, intolerant, impatient, sweaty, withdrawn, exhausted person who looks like mummy but is not the same.

As with all these conversations, find a time when you know it's quiet and your little one(s) will listen to you. That means no TV, gaming console, telephone and noisy toys. With little children you have a very small window of concentration, so it's important to plan what you are going to say and how you are going to say it. Their attention span is naturally very short. Don't be too adult or complex, even if they are super-bright. They won't get it. Remember, this is a new concept about something they don't understand, and it's emotional because it affects mummy and them.

ADMISSION IS PROGRESS

You are not defending your corner. This is not a fight. Take a long, hard look at yourself. What are your extreme and not-so-extreme behaviours that have either turned up or become more prevalent?

What symptoms cause you the deepest pangs of guilt or remorse?

Look back at your list of symptoms in Chapter 1. How do your symptoms manifest themselves? Do you fly off the handle, shout or point fingers, are you suddenly spiteful, jealous or bear a grudge? Do you burst into tears over the slightest thing, sobbing uncontrollably, or maybe withdraw into a dark place and are unable to communicate or be present?

It is important to note that this is not an opportunity to give yourself a good kicking. Having said this, your children do not deserve it either; they are simply being children.

Be clear with yourself: how do your symptoms manifest as your 'Menopause Monster' and what do they look like?

WHAT ARE YOUR TRIGGERS?

We all have things that our children do that drive us crazy, that seem to hit a 'nerve' every time. During Menopause, due to the range and severity of symptoms, those 'nerves' seem to be sitting very close to the surface and quite possibly multiplied.

If you are tired or exhausted, stressed, ache all over, or suffering from anxiety, then most things will trigger a reaction. Often there is a chain of events that triggers a response.

Work backwards and ask yourself what happened just before the event and keep asking until you uncover what is really going on. You are plotting the chronology of your symptom in this environment with your children, just as you did for triggers in **You Now.**

It is important to clarify whether you lost your sense of proportion because you stepped on a piece of Lego or a discarded piece of banana in bare feet, which – let's face it – is never pleasant. Or maybe you haven't had a decent night's sleep for over a month.

You are not a saint. You are a woman who is pretty damn amazing, doing the best job she can. That is enough.

CALL MENOPAUSE BY ITS NAME

Start off by giving examples of when your symptoms were out of control, discussing them in simple language that you didn't mean to act that way or that there is no need to worry and that it wasn't their fault.

Explain that Menopause is a grown-up female thing and that you can't always control it, although you are doing your best. I have always found that calling it 'Menopause Monster' makes it something they understand instantly. It is a concept that all children can identify with and something that is separate to you that your children can hang your behaviours from. Maybe even consider buying something that you agree looks like a Menopause Monster as a reference point.

This level of separation will be invaluable as you move into your post-Menopausal years. It will enable you and them to leave that person or set of behaviours behind. Goodbye, Menopause Monster.

MAINTAINING THE RELATIONSHIP

Keep talking often. Remember, you are giving them a way to keep seeing you as the mummy you know you are.

GET THEM TO CALL YOUR 'MENOPAUSE MONSTER' OUT

I am not going to lie to you; this can be difficult to do. If an adult tells you that you are being unreasonable when you are at the pinnacle of your outburst, it can and usually does end badly. No matter how much you love them. So, giving your children permission to call you out might seem crazy. But by giving them permission you are effectively giving them and, in turn you, control. Make it into a game; maybe they can call it when they see the Menopause Monster coming out. It's less accusatory and more fun for them and can break the intensity of the moment for you. They can wave their Monster toy at you.

In order to make this work, you will need to recognize that this is not swords drawn for battle but an opportunity to show how valuable, observant and all-round-fabulous your children are. You are not asking them to be carers. You are asking them to be a loving early warning system that can stop any escalation to full-scale confrontation.

When you have subsequently calmed down, commend them. Tell them how amazing they are and how much they helped. For this to work, though, you do need to stop the escalation in its tracks, no matter how hard that is. If you don't, it will be pointless and make your children powerless in the face of a monster. I am not saying that this is easy but responding to your children's observations will benefit you both in the long run.

Lastly, call on your partner if you have one for help. If you don't, call on your support network. There is no shame in saying you need to walk around the block to clear your head, or someone else to occupy the kids while you go and do something for yourself. Taking some time for yourself is allowed. Obviously, never leave your children alone or unattended or leave them with others for an extended period.

WHAT TO DO IF IT DETERIORATES

Take action.

If you have young children and your symptoms are escalating out of control, you will need to seek additional help. Visit your GP to discuss your options or, alternatively, find a registered Menopause specialist via the British Menopause Society.

Having young children at this time in life can be complex, but the problems are not insurmountable. At the heart of this is your love for them – hang on to that when all around you seems out of control. In effect, it will give you safe harbour throughout your Menopause. The monsters will give up. Like the tiger who came to tea,[49] it won't be back.

SUCCESSFUL 'M' CONVERSATIONS WITH OLDER CHILDREN

There is some overlap here with the chapter on communicating with younger children. That is because you are likely to be reading only one. If you have both younger and older children and are looking for advice on both, there are points of difference to warrant reading both – but please excuse the similarities.

You are likely to be experiencing your Menopause at a time when your children are either becoming, or are, young adults. This is a time that presents its own challenges with the need for more independence on both your parts, while still wanting to keep your baby safe and close before they leave the nest or at least take their first tentative steps.

CLASH OF THE HORMONAL TITANS

This would be an emotionally tumultuous time even without two sets of competing hormones: yours on the way out and theirs on the way in. Cue tears, shouting and door slamming.

Older children, while more able to verbalize their dismay, will feel confused or at times betrayed by a parent who is both different and inconsistent. All of this can come at a time in their lives when they are facing increasingly complex challenges.

Most mothers of teenagers or young adults whom I have spoken to say that this is a time that their children seem to need them more than ever, while conversely wanting to feel adult independence. This flip-flopping can be emotionally exhausting. Add this to your symptoms, and it can be even more so, creating extreme responses. I once worked with a woman who was distraught after losing all perspective and had screamed "f**k off" at her teenage son. She rarely swore, let alone in front of her children.

It can be extremely tough to hear or read that you are being unreasonable, but to admit that you are being this way with your children can be devastating. After all, you have surely made it through the hard bit of parenting. It seems somewhat unfair that you are now faced with your own hormonal changes causing a nagging anxiety that you are never quite good enough as a mother. It is another lose-lose situation.

You may have spoken to your children about personal issues before, both for them and for you. If you haven't, it's a bit of a cold standing start, but one that is necessary.

ADMISSION IS PROGRESS

The first thing to say here is that you are not defending your corner. Retaliation or defence only makes things worse. Even though they may be as confrontational as an adult, they are still your children and you love them. This activity is not about winners or losers but about empathy and understanding. Take a long, hard look at yourself: what are your extreme and not-so-extreme behaviours that have either turned up or become more prevalent?

What causes you those deep pangs of guilt or remorse?

Go back to Chapter 1 and be clear with yourself about how and when your symptoms show up. If you find yourself shifting in your seat uncomfortably, don't panic – this is not an opportunity to give yourself a good kicking. Having said this, your children do not deserve it either; they are simply trying to forge their own identity.

WHAT ARE YOUR TRIGGERS?

Older children have more sophisticated and complex ways of hitting our buttons, but there is usually a well-worn process and outcome to what they do. They know that if they do x, then you do y. During Menopause, due to the range and severity of symptoms, those 'nerves' or 'buttons' seem to be sitting very close to the surface and multiplied.

Just as with younger children, you need to understand what the chronology and triggers are when you are with your children, just like you did in **You Now**. You are now working at a micro level.

Work backwards, ask yourself what happened just before the event and keep asking until you uncover what is really going on.

It is important to clarify whether you lost your sense of proportion because their bedroom smells like a hamster's cage or because you haven't had a decent night's sleep in months.

Be kind to yourself; you are a woman who is pretty damn amazing, doing the best job she can. That is enough.

CALL IT BY ITS NAME – 'MENOPAUSE'

Start off by giving examples of when your symptoms were out of control or when your behaviour was the polar opposite of what would have once been normal. Apologize, explain that this is your Menopause, that the hormones that have been playing havoc with their body over the last few years are doing just the same to you as they start to make their exit. If they have questions or comments, be prepared to listen.

However, this is not a time when either of you has the right to ridicule, belittle or be hurtful toward each other. If the conversation is heading down a well-worn path toward an argument, stop it there, take a break and return to it later. Having said this, most women find that their children are simply relieved that mum is still in there somewhere and that you are not ill.

If you are lucky enough to have children who have been educated in a woman's full hormonal life, celebrate it.

GIVE THEM PERMISSION TO CALL IT OUT

Giving your children permission to call you out might seem crazy, especially as they are young adults. It seems to spark the defence mechanism much more quickly. Often, we are unaware in that moment that we are escalating out of control. It is only on reflection that we recognize the extreme nature of our behaviour. By giving them permission, you are getting an independent set of eyes and ears looking out for you, effectively giving them – and, in turn, you – control of the escalation of your symptoms and the ability to offset the remorse that often follows.

MAINTAINING THE RELATIONSHIP

Keep talking, keep listening. This is a time when mutual understanding and empathy is critical. Recognizing this will help you when the tears and tantrums are at their worst. That's yours and theirs. They won't have expected their mum to act in a similar way to themselves. You'll be on 'their patch'.

By giving your children the permission to call you out when your behaviours are escalating, you must listen to them when they do. If you don't, it can cause bitterness, cynicism and mistrust just at the time you need it least.

You are going to have to lead by example with adult and adaptive behaviours, because you are teaching your children behavioural codes that they will take into their adult lives. Value their openness to help you and support you. Commend them for having the courage to step in. Lastly, thank them for loving you.

This is a complex time for you and your children. All of you are prone to extreme and irrational behaviour and you are, possibly for the first time, showing that you are vulnerable. You are, after all, a human with a full set of emotions. Your children are also on their long journey into adulthood.

WHAT TO DO IF IT DETERIORATES

Take action.

Your children cannot divorce or fire you, but they are drawing close to a time when they can leave. Neither of you want it to happen just yet, so don't let it.

This is a critical time in your children's development. They need the security of home, and they need to know that they are loved unquestioningly. If your symptoms are affecting either or both, you need to call in your support network to help you.

First, if you have a partner, they need to stand beside you. You are a team and need to work as one. Create strategies to reconnect as a family unit. You and your partner may have disagreements over strategy, language and content in private, but always maintain a unified position with your children.

Call upon your wider family group. There have been numerous studies that say aunts and uncles are particularly important during puberty.[50] They are semi-independent yet trusted adult reference points. It will enable both of you to feel supported.

Finally, visit your GP to talk about symptom management options. Failing this, visit a registered Menopause specialist.

Whether your children are younger or older, talking about it is always the first thing to do. You will feel vulnerable and the stakes always feel impossibly high because of the emotions that are wrapped up in your children.

You will undoubtedly need to be the adult because you are the adult. I know this sounds obvious but some women in this moment of darkness become a child or a victim. They look to their children to rescue them, but they are children and don't have the resources to do so. Nor should they. Neither of these is helpful to your children or you. You may even need to ask your children to call you out on this if they sense you are moving into this position.

Be the one who keeps talking about it and maintain a loving bond. You will be grateful for the effort it took when you are post-Menopausal and out the other side.

CHAPTER 33
SUMMARY

WHAT WE LEARNED

The status that women have held in relationships has only started to change relatively recently. We have long been seen as being tied to the kitchen, in service of our husbands and our family. Our work has been seen as menial and generally low paid, if at all. These preconceptions are imbedded within our lifetimes and, as such, require us to define a new understanding and method of interaction.

Most women stoically soldiered on, managing Menopausal symptoms on their own with little or no support or empathy from their partners or the medical profession. Expectations have now changed. Yet we still find that Menopause challenges us as intelligent women, partners and as mothers.

We looked at how the myriad of changes during Menopause can affect our sense of desire and desirability. We considered that the emotional, psychological and physical effects of Menopause can have a profound effect on our ability to be intimate.

WHAT WE DID

We prepared for the 'M' conversation with our partners and children by referring back to the work we did in earlier chapters – recognizing our symptoms, their interdependency, and how and when they show up. All of this enabled us to say specifically what our symptoms are, what Menopause feels like on the inside and how that affects our behaviours.

We navigated the complex and vulnerable nature of discussing Menopause with those we love, admitting our need for support and asking for and receiving it – and recognizing that they need the reassurance of knowing that you are not only all right, but that you will surface from this experience at some point in the future.

We gave them the permission and the means to call you out when your behaviour starts to escalate, giving you both control over your experience together.

We faced the taboo inside the taboo – vaginal dryness and atrophy – and understood how common it is, and what to do when it occurs.

We passed this book to our partners so that they could get a better understanding of our experience and our needs during this phase of life. This led to the process of starting to plan together to gain a clear vision of joint ambitions for the next five years.

HOW THIS HELPS

Your preparedness to be vulnerable and discuss your symptoms and changes in your behaviours with your loved ones will ensure you maintain the trust and empathy between you. It draws them into your sphere of understanding and enables them to gain a little insight into what you are wrestling with. In doing so, this gives you all perspective and control.

Recognizing that your intimate relationship is complex and comes under pressure at this time helps both of you talk openly about ways to mitigate it. Sex is something that you experience together; therefore, the solutions to any issues that arise need to be jointly appreciated.

Your relationship with your children is incredibly precious and, as such, talking to them about your Menopause whether they are young or older draws them closer to you. It reverses the potential to inadvertently alienate them due to unexplained behaviour changes.

Planning gives you and your partner the ability to take control of what happens next. This can be critical at a time of instability.

Part V

NEW

CHAPTER 34

YOUR NEW RELATIONSHIP: INTRODUCTION

I f you find yourself single at the time of your Menopause, you are in the perfect position to reassess not only the life you would like to lead, but who you would like to share it with. You are effectively creating two new beginnings at the same time – one you have not been in control of and one where you are. It is a fantastic opportunity to recognize the you that is emerging and to value the woman you are becoming.

I found my husband in my very late 30s. One of my bosses had said, "Who would want you?" when everyone was discussing their partners and families. It surfaced that I was single and had been for a very long time. Everyone laughed nervously, while I wept somewhere deep inside. The problem was, I was actually starting to believe that my undesirability in all its dimensions was true.

I attracted a wide range of idiots, users and bad boys. Amid the losers, I did love once, but it wasn't to be. While I mourned its failure, my apparent options and choices descended at high speed to the bottom of the pool, where I bumped blindly along. This would likely have stayed the same until I made some profound decisions. Once I did, I changed and, as if by magic, so did my options.

When looking to start again, it is imperative that you recognize who you are today and who you might be tomorrow. You need to remove any ingrained self-imposed stereotypes that you have harboured, as well as any damaging judgments from yourself or others about who you are becoming. You literally start again.

In this chapter, we are considering new relationships during Menopause. We will look at societal stereotypes and gender-based prejudice and how they impact us as we seek to find a new partner during this phase of our lives. We consider how dating has changed over the last two decades with the advent of online resources, and we evaluate the importance of attraction via your mind before your body.

As this is about you finding a partner that fulfils you, we start with you. That is, how you view yourself and the impact this has on both you and your ability to attract someone who will inspire you. We discuss the importance of values and how they play a pivotal role in trust and connection.

Next, we investigate your hidden superpower, your brain, and how it continuously seeks to find what you want. By giving it enough detailed instructions, it will seek to fulfil your requirements.

We wave the red flag at some of the unwanted types of partners we might come across, how to identify them and what to do when you do: walk away, quickly.

We look at intimacy, because it's important both for you and your prospective partner. By recognizing that desire is complex and is reliant on more than your hormones, you can take control and implement change or seek support as necessary.

Unlike the other sections of this book, for new relationships there is likely to be a time when you don't want to have the 'M' conversation, whether that be because of the negative societal preconceptions and stereotypes previously discussed or simply because it feels too personal. Gauging when that changes can be important for the success of your fledgling connection. But at some point you will need to raise it and, just as in earlier sections we look at the preparation, the conversation itself, maintaining the relationship and the conversation, and what to do if things deteriorate.

There is some overlap in this section with the last because, after all, we are discussing intimate relationships, but this is kept to a minimum as the conditions are not only different but newly formed and require gentle consideration.

New relationships after Menopause is over are a different challenge entirely, but one that having honed your resources in this transitory phase, you will be more than able to meet.

CHAPTER 35
CONTEXT: SOCIETY

Being single through divorce or separation during Menopause is a relatively modern experience. This means you are in the position where you need to create your own positive narrative. There is little to build on. Historically, our societal expectations were that we would remain married until our husbands sadly passed and then remain single unless we had the good fortune to meet someone, usually depicted as kindly and without expectations, to look after us. Of course, many women were widowed by WWI and WWII, yet widows – then and more recently – fared only marginally better in social depiction or expectation as far as behaviours were concerned.

For those women who had children, being single and without a partner to work and provide for them was extremely hard, no matter how they came to be single. Women's work was considered menial and, therefore, poorly paid. Childcare outside of family structures did not exist.

For those of us who had mothers who were single, there was general social condemnation. You were likely to be excluded from social gatherings, as wives or existing partners were nervous that their husbands or partners would be lured away by promises of free and easy sex. Of course, this is the ultimate irony from the generation that brought us swinging, key parties[51] and the joy of sex.[52]

Being gay, while not historically illegal for women, was still viewed negatively in the wider social context. The 1960s saw the development of political lesbianism and feminism, which promoted lesbianism positively. Considerable advancement in the awareness and acceptance of lesbianism was achieved. Yet, for many women not from liberal or educated backgrounds, the opportunity to openly express their sexuality was still extremely limited and fraught with prejudice and disadvantage.

Our collective drive to independence, via education and successful careers, has meant our economic influence on society and its limiting prejudices and stereotypes has been eroded more due to commerciality than acceptance. How, where and when we choose to spend our money has attracted attention and big corporations are watching closely. They now know that they must appear inclusive with positive female imaging ... in the majority.

If we choose to be single, it is just that – a choice. We can pay our own rent or mortgage, we can feed and clothe ourselves and our children if we have them. We no longer need to be beholden to a partner who doesn't fulfil us or make our heart skip a beat. Equally, we don't need to settle for someone who is less than we would hope for.

STEREOTYPES

For centuries, Menopausal and post-Menopausal women have been seen in a negative light. Past our prime. Our dewy youthfulness gone, our ripeness for reproduction over.

Society often viewed women over the age of 45 who were dating as desperate. Charity cases who should be pitied. We were 'left on the shelf', 'spinsters' or, worst of all, 'old maids'. We were also seen as frenzied individuals who teetered on the verge of being 'bunny boilers'.[53] We were isolated, separate, different, possibly even dangerous as in Greek mythology's Sirens, luring innocent and potentially not so innocent individuals to our lair.

Not anymore.

The highest rate for heterosexual divorce[54] among women is in the 40–44 age group and 45–49 age group for men. Same-sex marriage is too new of a legal institution to predict. You are, therefore, in good company. Admittedly the pool of suitable men or women is considerably smaller than it was when you were a teenager, but that is not necessarily a bad thing. It concentrates the mind on what you want rather than what passed you by. This is not the conveyor belt on *The Generation Game*.[55] "Didn't she do well?"

INEQUALITY TO EQUALITY

While women are often viewed negatively as they get older, the view of men has been the opposite. Men have been seen as mature, distinguished and accomplished. In dating terms, this means that men see the entire scope of womanhood as potential partners and are positively applauded should they choose a 'younger model'. This is insulting.

This is a view that is created by men to support men's poor behaviour. The reality is, you are unlikely to have a successful relationship with a man who is needing to affirm with himself that he is still able to attract a much-younger woman. That is, unless you yourself like older men. You are not a nanny looking after a little boy. You are an adult, seeking another adult to spend significant time with.

You are at a point where you can define what you like and what you want. To be open to new experiences whatever they may be. In today's gender-fluid world, you may choose to love either a woman or a man. You set the rules. Not society.

CHAPTER 36
CONTEXT: DATING

When you were young, you met potential dates at college, in the local bar, nightclub or round at your mates' house party. It was generally fine if you didn't meet someone one week or month because you might very well the next.

If you were single in your 20s or 30s, you generally met dates at work or while socializing with colleagues in a city bar, or if you went to the gym or at the club you were a member of.

Of course, there were the personal ads at the back of newspapers and costly dating agencies at the back of women's magazines.

I tried the latter at my mother's insistence. It was an unmitigated disaster. I sat with my heart in my heels as I looked at the person who was meant to be my date. *Surely*, I thought, *I could do better than this*. It seemed not. Every other prospective date cancelled with minutes to spare or was over 30 years my senior and thinking about their pension. Profile and reality were poles apart. My expectations and reality were a similar distance.

The last 15 to 20 years has seen the explosion of internet dating and internet 'hook-up' applications – shagging to you and me.

ONLINE

Online dating has many advantages. There are quite literally tens of thousands of potential dates available. Chance is close to eliminated. We know something about them before we engage (whether it's true or not is another matter). There is also a site for every type of sexual preference or niche conceivable.

You can apply to the exclusive sites that require you to earn a certain amount, be a certain grade of executive, or have a certain level of education or intellect.

As with everything, it's not all good. You must be prepared for the bad side, too. It is important to remember that this level of choice works both ways; you are also one of tens of thousands of women seeking a relationship. It's why people spend so much time on their profiles and their pictures. Sadly, it's why so many lie. If they seem too good to be true, they invariably are. This means the ones who are good tend not to be believed.

Just as with all social media, people behave badly. There is little you can do about it and the lack of proximity means that people feel no discomfort when being unnecessarily harsh to another person. It is fairly cut-throat in that people don't respond or literally cut you off if they don't want to speak to you, decide they are not interested in you or receive a better offer. At least on screen. Having said this, don't let it put you off. It doesn't mean you shouldn't try; many people extol its virtues. Just don't assume it's a panacea.

CHANCE ENCOUNTERS

These still happen, honest.

I think the main thing to realize is that you shouldn't rely on it. Expecting a thunderbolt or Cupid's arrow is a unicorn moment.

I remember sitting in a café one morning and seeing a man in his late 50s stop in his tracks as he turned and saw a woman of similar age, who was sat laughing with a friend. She saw him and smiled. He tripped over a chair on his way out and stood outside trying to gather himself, not knowing what to do.

The problem with relying on chance encounters is they are akin to fairy tales. These tales are based on historical social constructs to limit women's expectations and remove their belief that they are the ones who define their future. You are a grown woman; you have made your own way in the world. To believe that your hero is about to arrive on their trusty steed is naïve. It is also damaging because, in effect, you are saying that someone has control over you and your future life. The only person who has control is you. Don't give it away, even in a fantasy.

MIND, THEN BODY, THEN SOUL

There is an order of play.

Whether you meet someone by swiping right or by serendipity, it is important that you connect mentally before it becomes physical. You are an intelligent, capable woman. Honour this part of yourself first. Your mind and your mental abilities have worked incredibly hard on your behalf up until this point. They underpin your lifestyle, your job and your aspirations. To put them to the back of the queue is disrespectful to you. You wouldn't sell yourself short at work, so don't do it here.

Physical attraction is incredibly important, but your body is changing, and you may find that you feel different about being intimate with someone. We will cover this in greater detail a little later. Needless to say, there are things you can do.

Finding that deeper connection to someone is incredibly important and rare. It takes time. Only you will know if you have it. Be aware of self-deception, though. If all the soul and chemistry is coming from you, this is not, and never will be, a successful relationship. Contrary to popular depiction, you cannot love someone enough for both of you – no matter how much you want this to be true.

When you have all three in harmony, you will have found something truly amazing.

CHAPTER 37
YOU

Before you turn on your technology or dig out your favourite outfit, it's important to start with you. In **You Now** and **Future You**, you identified where you are now and where you want to be in the future. We have dealt in detail with your relationship with yourself, those you work with and your children, if you have them. It is also important to be clear about your health, fitness and finances, because they underpin who you are and the lifestyle you either lead or aspire to. All of this is critical when seeking a partner. What do you think about yourself when you look in the mirror? Do you like the version of you that stands before you or do you not? If you think positively about yourself then, unsurprisingly, so will others and vice versa.

If you are rooted in who you are and what you are about, you will find that connection easier to seek and identify when it occurs.

YOUR VIEW OF YOURSELF

In **Future You**, when you dreamed big, were you happy every-where with your lot except in love and intimacy, or were there areas that you wanted it to be different no matter how small? In your five- and ten-year plan, you were asked, "If everything were to be just as you liked it, it would be like what?" Go back and look at your answer. What was your vision of yourself and for yourself – were you active, sporty, bookish, super-sociable? Were you focusing on your career, in whichever direction that was? All these answers feed into the type of person you are becoming and the type of person you need to meet you in the middle, to share both good times and bad.

It seems obvious, but recognizing your needs comes first. If you have a specific pastime that you love, your prospective partner will either need to support you as you pursue it, or they will already love it or grow to appreciate it. Whether you have a passion for running marathons or doing macramé, recognize the acceptance you need from a prospective partner.

Below is a table for you to complete. It will help you to clarify your favourite pastimes and your most fulfilling social activities.

When I have time to do as I want, I like to ...
1. ...
2. ...
3. ...

I am at my happiest when I ...	
1.	...
2.	...
3.	...
When I socialize, I like to ...	
1.	...
2.	...
3.	...

Now you have a clearer picture of what is important. It will also help you identify the best dating sites to register with should you wish to go down this route.

VALUES

Values are often hidden from view, yet they underpin the way we behave and interact with others. They are present in society and the community we live in, the family we grew up in, the companies we work for and, unsurprisingly, ourselves. We may develop opposing values to our family or community, or we may perpetuate them. They govern what we will and won't do.

Values are so important that companies spend considerable sums of money identifying them and effectively (or usually ineffectively) communicating them to their staff and customers. Whole books have been written about them, and many dating sites now ask you to stipulate your values.

They are an industry of their own.

Values are so important because we identify with them at a deeper, more subconscious level. When others' values match our own, we trust people and feel connected to them. For corporates, that trust means that we spend our precious time and/or money with them and, very importantly, we continue to do so. Politicians seek to convey their values so that we believe them and vote for them.

The potential list of values is vast. These tend to be words based on actions and interactions. For example: kindness, winning, tenacity, openness, tolerance, sincerity, honesty and compassion. Most of us, given the opportunity, would say that many are important; however, there will be some that resonate more deeply with you than others.

There is a difference between a value – something you hold absolute – and something you value. You may value punctuality, but it is not a value. Values will change with you over time and are subject to the phase of your life, your situation or the wider environment. Some may stay the same, but others change as we do.

For some, the concept of personal values is a new one. The following table[56] has a list of some of the more common values to assist you in your thinking.

Bravery	Leadership
Creativity	Love
Citizenship	Love of learning
Curiosity	Open mindedness
Fairness	Perspective
Forgiveness	Persistence
Gratitude	Prudence
Hope	Self-regulation
Humility	Social intelligence
Humour	Spirituality
Integrity	Vitality
Kindness	Wonder

Remember, when thinking about your values, they are not the things you would like to demonstrate to the world. They are knitted into your very being and are at the core of your behaviours, they drive how you are in the world. Like it or not, they are demonstrated in everything you do.

Values are at their most powerful when we live them. Our behaviour matches what we believe in and hold to be important. If we claim to value honesty and yet are happy to tell the odd white lie, we probably don't value honesty quite as much as we say we do. Can you say what your values are now? Try to list five. You will find that one or two of these particularly resonate with you. They create a set of conditions that a prospective partner will need to honour.

My core values are:
1.   ...
2.   ...
3.   ...
4.   ...
5.   ...

Think about how you then live those values, and how they are reflected in your behaviours. Give some examples.

How I live my values	Examples
1. ...	...
2. ...	...
3. ...	...
4. ...	...
5. ...	...

Why is all this important? If your values are not met by another or worse, are trampled on by them, we can feel enraged, ostracized, separate or disconnected. If someone we love does this, it can make the relationship difficult or even impossible to be in. This is one of the reasons why honesty is so important for many couples, especially when they have experienced dishonesty or deception previously.

You will know if someone doesn't share your values. It will feel scratchy, uncomfortable, like someone has been eating toast in bed. Alternatively, you might simply dislike or mistrust them.

YOUR JUDGMENT

Throughout this book we have covered the changes that Menopause brings in your behaviour in detail and, in particular, your ability to judge situations in the manner you once did. When seeking a new relationship during your Menopause, your symptoms will affect the manner in which you assess and respond to situations. This is heightened by the added uncertainty that a potential new relationship brings.

If at this stage your confidence is low, you will likely snatch at decisions that you once may have been more careful with. If others let you down or do not appear as you had initially seen them, you may react in ways that ensure the situation cannot be rescued.

Therefore, it is hugely important to assess your Menopausal symptoms against the changing situations which you may find yourself in.

FROM THE OUTSIDE IN

I asked at the beginning of this section, "When you look in the mirror, do you like what you see?"

I am always saddened when women tell me that they have stopped looking in the mirror. Please note this is not the same as looking to check your teeth or your hair. This is proper, full on, looking in the mirror, one that is bigger than 30cm by 30cm, preferably full length. A stylist I know confers that there are more women than you think who leave the house without checking their appearance, from hair to soles. This is not vanity; this is positive self-appreciation.

Are you suddenly realizing that you are one of those people who doesn't have a full-length mirror at home or, if you do, it's on the inside of your wardrobe door that is conveniently always draped in clothes or scarves? When you use public toilets, do you choose the ones that have small mirrors or do you become scientifically interested in the process of hand washing and drying to avoid looking into the inconveniently placed wall-sized mirrors?

Self-loathing is incredibly damaging to you as an individual. What one thing do you like about yourself, perhaps throughout everything you ensured that you preserved it? Is it your hair, teeth, legs, bum or perhaps something a little more ethereal like your laugh, your smile, your wiggle? We all have something. The trick is to start with that and work your way out. While this could be an exercise in attraction, it is more for your own benefit. If you can anchor yourself in one thing that you feel is good about your physicality, it will enable you to build your own self-esteem outward from that point.

Our body language and speech patterns tell the world how we feel about ourselves. We tell people that we feel like crap or are disappointed in ourselves. The words have a way of slipping out, yet we don't even hear them. In addition to this, we slump, shy or turn away. We even spend much of our lives looking down, inspecting municipal paving. Our physiology tells people even – before we say a word – how we feel or what we think about ourselves. Therefore, starting with something that we feel great about enables us to speak positively or to physically redirect our eyes to something about us that lets us metaphorically stand tall and look up to meet our own gaze.

AGEING

There are few things in life that draw your advancing years into clearer view than your Menopause – varifocals notwithstanding. That is unless you have had a medical Menopause or POI. The loss of elasticity and plumpness, delivered by declining levels of oestrogen and collagen, means your body is showing the first early signs of sagging and loss of suppleness.

Your muscles are naturally lessening and, all in all, it can feel thoroughly disheartening. How the hell are we to compete with the 20-30-year olds now?

The truth is going to hurt. You can't, so don't try. Instead of swimming against the tide, which is pointless, knackering and even more disheartening, stop.

I love an anti-wrinkle cream, and I am a sucker for an anti-cellulite cream – none of them work, but I remain ever hopeful. I am also having to face the fact that I can't wear miniskirts without opaque tights to hide my increasingly unattractive knees. The list is long, and I am not especially enamoured with it.

It's time to 'circle the wagons' or 'make a square' – whichever film-based metaphor works best for you – and realize the following.

Obvious statement No. 1: Attractiveness is about you being you and loving it – whatever it happens to be.

Obvious statement No. 2: We are all ageing.

Obvious statement No. 3: If we are lucky enough to live that long, we will all be old one day.

Time is finite, so don't waste it on worrying about things you can't control. Instead, recognize who you are and would like to be, who you would like to meet, and focus on meeting them. Loving the life you have will enable you to take a more positive view of the issues surrounding the ageing process.

In the section above, you thought about what you like about your body. The table below is for the things you appreciate about your mind and your soul as well – that deep inner part of you that yearns to sing with another. This is a simple exercise, yet one that can be difficult, especially if you have been through emotional turmoil to get to this point and are managing a complex array of symptoms.

The things I appreciate most about me are ...		
Mind	Body	Soul
1. ...	...	...
2. ...	...	...
3. ...	...	...

Commending ourselves is not a skill often taught in many cultures and especially to women. Now is the time to begin. You really do have superpowers. It's time to dust them off and give them some recognition.

WEIGHING IN ... ON MENOPAUSE

Weight gain is a symptom of Menopause. We can't pretend it's not.

Many women find the sudden and seemingly inexplicable weight gain devastating to their confidence. It is all the more impactful for those women looking to find a new partner. All too often, women say that they don't feel sexy anymore, or that they feel so unhappy with their changing body that they would rather postpone dating until they manage to lose the pounds. Sadly, this often means women needlessly become lonely. Action is required, and only you can choose to take it.

I know that this next section will be contentious, but I am compelled to say it because so many women gain weight during their Menopause. They naturally get distressed about it. If you are happy with your body, by all means skip this part. If you are not, whether it's for health or self-esteem reasons, read on.

As oestrogen production in your ovaries declines, your body seeks to produce it elsewhere. Fat produces oestrogen, and belly fat is particularly good at producing oestrogen. Your body will endeavour to add fat all over your body and especially around your middle, in order to fulfil its needs. Combined with a natural fall in your metabolism, this means that you will need to take greater action to lose weight than you have done before. Just saying 'no' to the mid-morning biscuit fest or afternoon doughnut-a-rama, while positive, will not be enough. There are plenty of options out there, and you need to choose whichever suits you best.

I confess, I was one of those women. In my first 12 months as a post-Menopausal woman, I piled on 10kg. This was on top of the 3-4kg I had gained over the previous four years that I was kidding myself I could lose (tomorrow, naturally). To give you some context, I had always been tall, relatively slim and curvy. I had taken part in competitive sport since an early age and never stopped. I had sweated off my considerable baby weight after both of my daughters were born and always felt in control.

As I stood on the scales dreading the number I would be faced with, I watched them increase as though they were on fruit-machine reels. I tried all my usual tactics, but nothing helped. I had two questions: when would this end? And how could I stop it?

The turning point occurred when I met a woman for a business lunch. I had spent the preceding hours trying on all my business clothes to find that I could no longer get into any of them. That is not strictly true; I could get into them, I just couldn't do them up. I stared at my bulging figure, horrified and somewhat desperate. I simply didn't know what to do. I settled on a pair of black trousers that I had bought after my first daughter was born. I would have to discreetly undo them when I sat down and hope that my burgeoning backside would be contained by the forgiving wool crepe. I chose a ridiculously patterned bright shirt, simply because it contained elastane, which meant I could do it up. I hoped that the pattern would hide my rolls of back- and everything-else fat.

On my way to the meeting, I went to a department store to buy an outfit for a forthcoming event. I stared at myself in numerous sequined outfits, wondering if they sold smocks in my size. Sparkly earrings were not going to be enough to distract people's attention or my own self-loathing. I needed a miracle. The lady I met for lunch was it. Nearly a year later, I am 12kg lighter. If you are reading this, thank you. You have been – and remain – an inspiration.

There are countless methods to lose weight, and you need to choose one that's right for you. As stated, losing weight at this age requires focus, conviction and, above all, obsessive commitment. Breaking the rules 'just this once' leads to 'a little bit of what you like does no harm' and before you know it, you are back where you started.

There will be low times, when all you want to eat is chips, pizza or chocolate or perhaps all three. You will need to be resolutely committed to your path to remain on it. To help you through this, be ruthlessly honest with yourself. To prompt you, answer the following questions. Write the answers down and keep them; it will help to keep you honest with yourself.

Why are you doing this?

What are your motivations – has there been a tipping point?

How will you know you are making progress? Lots of small targets make the big success easy.

For it to be like that, you will be like what?

This is not about being 'model' thin; it's about feeling great about your body and equally about feeling in control. This process will give you a sense of power. Stepping out with this sense rather than a negative self-image will be like a magnet to those you wish to attract. Feeling good about yourself inside and out is a superpower. It is waiting to be claimed. So, claim it.

CHAPTER 38
BRAIN GAMES

Your brain is an amazing thing for lots of reasons, not least because it is continuously working on your behalf. Your brain never stops looking to fulfil the instructions you give it. Whatever you tell your brain, it will look to find it for you. Yes, it really is true. Your brain is a superpower.

All too often, we amble blindly into the dating world, hoping that what we think we might want or like will be delivered to our door. Unfortunately, thought-reading delivery systems are housed next to the sparkly unicorns, and they generally choose not to bother leaving the stables.

Momentary thoughts or hopes are not enough to instruct our brains to seek or find. This leaves us scrabbling to choose between the flotsam and jetsam that flows past. This is not choice; it is false hope desperation.

True choice requires you to know what it is that you want, ranging from absolute must-haves to the jam and cream should it be offered.

This section gets your brain working for you. It truly is astounding once you point it in the right direction.

FILTRATION SYSTEMS

The level of information our brains receive in a single moment is immense. It has information from all our senses in fabulous technicolour with full surround sound, more smells than the Selfridges' perfume department, tastes from delicious to disgusting, and touch and all its fabulous delights. Realistically, all this is far too much for us to deal with in its minutiae. There are 100 million bits of information coming in every second through your visual (eye) system, another 10 million bits coming through your auditory (hearing) system and another one million bits coming through your tactile (touch) system.[57]

As humans, the way we have evolved to cope with this is that we have created customized filters that effectively park huge sections of information, only allowing key pieces through. We refine our filters over time to section off the things we have told ourselves are not essential. We don't even think about it. It just happens subconsciously. The signals are filtered from the noise. There are a lot less signals than noise. What we pay attention to gets laid down as stronger, more accessible neural pathways – meaning we then travel those pathways more often, making them stronger still.

Therein lies the issue. It is up to us to modify our filters as we change. If you have not recently reviewed who or what it is that you like and desire, then your filters are likely to be seeking what you thought was attractive the last time you were dating. Even if that was a fairly recent event, it's likely it won't be up to date. Given this, your brain could be overlooking potential opportunities.

For example, have you ever chosen something because you thought it was rare or unique, only to find that it sprung up everywhere? That is your brain seeking and finding what you have focused on. You changed your filters, and your brain did the rest.

Now is the time to make sure you know what you want. Once you have defined it, your brain will busy itself in the background, like your very own personalized matchmaker.

RALEIGH CHOPPER OR A CRISP COLD CAVA

You are not the same as you were when you were 11, 21 or even 31. Your tastes have probably changed. I am sure most of us didn't even know what a cappuccino was until 20 years ago, let alone any of the other coffee variations we take for granted today. I can't remember seeing an avocado or a mango during my early adulthood, either. I remember quizzing a waiter in Paris over the flavour of a blueberry. How the world has changed.

My point here, other than the fact that my eating habits have changed, is that as we grow up, our perceptions change as we experience things. We become more complex as our understanding of life – both good and bad – affects us.

When you were 11, you might have thought that a Raleigh Chopper bicycle was the height of finesse, while in your 20s it might have been shoulder pads. Your 30s might have kicked off with Pinot Grigio after work in a wine bar, while your 40s saw you familiarize yourself with champagne or cava when you didn't feel quite so flush. Likewise, hanging around outside the local chippy probably doesn't have the same allure as it used to. Go back to the table you filled in called **Your view of yourself** and look at that in conjunction with your five- and ten-year plan to see what kind of partner you are looking for.

SUCCESS IS IN THE DETAIL

Your brain needs detail to ensure it does seek out what you really want. Your filters need to be specific.

When I ask them what they want, many women declare that they wish to be happy. I haven't yet heard anyone say that they wanted to be unhappy. Yet happiness is unique to each of us. What makes me happy is not the same as what makes you happy.

Happy is also too oblique a word for your brain; it isn't quite sure what you mean. Happy is extremely contextual. If I am thirsty, cold sparkling mineral water makes me extremely happy. The happiness derived from the water is obviously different to the happiness inside a loving and supportive relationship. Being specific and contextual is critical.

By giving your brain this level of detail, you are giving it a description it can work to. You are priming yourself to first experience it and second, know when you do.

The other important information is about the person you would like to meet. Be specific about their attributes, characteristics and values, how they make you feel when you are with them, what you might do together – including sex, but not just sex. What pastimes will you have together and separately? This is a great opportunity; don't waste it by skipping this step. If you don't use your considerable ability to recognize that your needs are important, to the degree that they need to be validated, you are exposing yourself to wasters and users. I've not only been there, done that and got the T-shirt, I had a wardrobe full.

The cold hard truth of the matter is that if you don't value you, nobody else will.

FOCUS ON YOUR POSITIVE REALITY

Without getting too woo-woo, you create your own reality. Whatever you focus on is your reality. Therefore, if you walk round permanently mulling over the vitriol that defined the end of your last relationship, things are not going to go well.

By this stage in life, we all have a history. Most of us have experienced heartache, bitterness, regret and disappointment. It comes with the territory. But carrying it around with you like Jacob Marley from Charles Dickens' A Christmas Carol is exhausting, and it doesn't support you in having a great relationship in the future. You are required to make a conscious decision to move on and relinquish or make peace with your past hurts.

The caveat here is if you are a widow. The agony of loss is incredibly deep and final. There is no animosity or vitriol replacing a once-cherished love. Those emotions are likely levelled at others or something higher than yourself. Moving on is not about relinquishing them but finding a place where they can sit beside you, knowing that they would not want you to be lonely or to live a life of solitude.

Creating a positive image in your mind of successfully dating a great person who is interesting, fun to be with, sexy and – above all – treats you with respect, will enable your brain to find them and prime you to achieve it.

With this in mind, the table below has some questions to help you. You know the process because you answered them before in **Future You**.

Vision	
For dating to be just the way I'd like it, it will be like what?	... **A**
When it's like [**A**] is there anything else about [**A**]?	...
For it to be like that, I'll be like what?	...

What will I see/hear when it's like [**A**]?	...
How will I know it's like [**A**]?	...

Who	
For it to be like that, they'll be like what?	... B
What will I see/hear when they're like [**B**]?	...
How will I know they're like [**B**]?	...
What will others see/hear when it's like [**A** and **B**]?	...
What support or resources will I need to make this happen?	...

CHAPTER 39
RED FLAGS

While it is important to focus on your desired outcomes, you still need to recognize that there are those you would rather not date. Unpleasant or untrustworthy individuals do not disappear when they get to their 40s. Some work it out of their system, some acquire it over time or through experience. If anything, suddenly returning to the dating market after an acrimonious split can cause people to behave more poorly than they would have previously. This is often driven by a need to make up for lost time or to transfer some of the dislike they feel for their previous partner onto others.

I get a fairly polarized response when I speak about this. Women either fall into the camp of those who have been burned by these individuals or those who find it unbelievable to think that a woman of this age could be so naïve.

If you are in the first camp, the trick is to ensure you are not a repeat booker. While unlikely, for the second camp the mission is never be tempted to visit.

INTERNET BOTTOM-FEEDERS

The internet, while creating opportunity, also brings out the very worst behaviour.

The advent of internet dating means that many women overly rely on the initial interactions to decide if they will move forward with a relationship. Deception is easy at the end of a WiFi connection.

We tell our children not to trust people over social media; we tell them not to reveal personal details and to keep all online interactions in proportion so that they don't spend every waking hour getting likes or distressing themselves over the lack of them. If only we played by the same rules.

Online dating is a shield for some. If someone hasn't got the depth of personality to dump you in person or by phone if you don't live nearby, then forget them. 'Ghosting', as this practice is called, is harsh and spineless on their part. They are not who you thought they were. Move on.

If someone flirts and then disappears, then returns to flirt or possibly even meet for a noncommittal shag and disappears again, all the signs were out in neon, telling you to say no when you blindfolded yourself and said yes. They are simply manipulating you, giving you just enough to want more. Move on and don't look back.

CHEATERS AND WASTERS

If someone cheats on you, wastes your time, says they'll turn up and doesn't, turns up late or drunk or displays any other ingenuine behaviours, take the scales from your eyes and see them for the utter waste of time that they are.

White lies are still lying, no matter how you dress them up. Stand tall, shoulders back, laugh in their face and walk away. Once out of view, run. Most importantly, learn.

PETER PANS

We all have a little bit of Peter Pan inside us. We all want to remain forever young, but that is not the reality. This stage in life is the point at which those people who always seemed to defy the gravitational pull of ageing, while you seemed to be succumbing, will start to lose the battle. You are not Wendy. You are not the adult in the room who will enable them to stay childlike and bypass responsibility.

Equally, they do not get the right to be critical of you and your sensibilities. These people are toxic. It is easy to be deceived by them. They are generally fun and charismatic, yet they don't take accountability for the hurt they cause. You need someone who will treat you like the intelligent women you are. This means you need an adult, not a child masquerading in an adult's body. Get your metaphorical Hazchem suit on and move on.

NOT PLAYERS BUT 'REPLAYERS'

It's unlikely you will even get a sniff of one of these sorts of people, because they are looking to replay their youth and have it validated by a much younger woman. They want to feel that freedom and energy once more. Consequence-free. While understandable in its purest evolutionary form, I have had to hold myself back from a withering and derisory onslaught.

They may seem energetic and alluring. During Menopause we can crave the life-sized human wheatgrass shot that these people represent. The temptation is high, but resist you must.

Do not bother chasing them; it really isn't worth it. You will only demean yourself in the process. Step back, be yourself.

Allow room for a more deserving candidate. Energy doesn't channel in this way – the distance between you will be more evident, and you'll waste your energy trying to keep up. And all of this will simply be to flatter them.

Do not put your life on hold. You no longer have the luxury of waiting ten or 20 years for them to return to you as a more mature individual. I have known women who have done this only to find it never happens or one or another of them becomes ill or passes away. It is a waste of all that potential in their lives.

No woman deserves to be treated badly. Looking for a partner should be an exciting time, not purgatory. Look forward, think about who you are and what you want and get your superpower, your brain, on your side and working for you.

CHAPTER 40
INTIMACY

Whereas 30 years ago you may have thrown off your clothes without a care in the world – or in fact might have worked hard to keep them on, especially after a few pints of snakebite in the student union bar – you now feel guarded and more than a little worried simply at the thought of it.

We have already looked at why and how Menopause affects body shape and the resulting impact on your self-image.

Life, especially if you have had children or surgery, can negatively affect your body at a greater level than just vanity. Considerable changes in body shape and scarring may have occurred. If you have led a fairly sedentary life or one that overindulged, you may now look wistfully back at your willowy youthful self. Perhaps you are starting to notice the first calling cards of ageing which, as we have already discussed, is happening to us all.

Menopause can and does affect many women's libido, which is underpinned by their sense of desire and desirability. It is a variable picture. Many report that their sex drive feels non-existent. This is opposite to the way it used to be, when you felt yourself to be a sexual being, driven by a deeper need. It is possible that if this is you, your complete loss of desire for your previous partner is what caused you to be single.

Others, however, report that their libido is unaffected. Some lucky few declare that theirs has increased.

Your sense of desire and desirability is complex and is not simply a case of 'clothes off, let's go!' even if it used to be. How you feel about yourself and your body and the context in which you find yourself in is as influential as your hormones.

There are a vast array of influencers and disrupters at play here. Some you can take immediate control of; for others, it's not so easy.

INFLUENCERS

Unsurprisingly, your hormones hugely influence your sense of desire. There are three at play here. Oestrogen and progesterone, which we all know about, and testosterone, which we usually think of as a male hormone. Testosterone is present in women's bodies, and its decline can seriously affect our sex drive. If a lack of it is the problem, you will need to see a Menopause specialist, as most GPs will not prescribe it.

Negative body image is something that many of us struggle with. This is an area of influence that you most definitely have control over. I have already covered weight gain in this chapter, but there is also the influence of overindulgence due to stress, unhappiness or loss. Whatever your drivers are, you can take control, and you can be healthier and fitter starting now. Action here helps your mind as well as your body. You will feel powerful and sexier because of it.

The type of partner you choose is extremely important. If you need someone to handle you gently, then choose someone like that. Recognize your own needs and decide accordingly.

DISRUPTERS

We covered the disrupters in the Personal section – vaginal dryness, thrush and bacterial vaginosis, leakage and incontinence, hot flushes and flooding. While each is problematic for an existing relationship, they can be far more serious for one just forming – for both symptoms and the subject of conversation. What may have been mere disrupters are now potential destroyers. It's important you take proactive action for yourself.

VULNERABILITY

Exposing your body for the first time and possibly the second or third time to someone new is always awkward, but if you are physically different to the way you used to be, it can be extremely nerve-wracking.

Under any circumstances, this is not going to make you feel particularly sexy or turned on. It is a hurdle you will need to clear before you can proceed to the part where you are back in the groove.

Your new partner will not have been on the journey with you through ill health or childbearing. Unless it is something obvious, they will not be able to guess from looking at you in your best dress.

If you think you can wing it, and that they are adult enough to pay no attention to it, great. But if you are particularly concerned about something, it is probably a good idea to discuss it before you get to the naked stage. That way, you can reassure yourself and ensure that there is no awkwardness later.

BEING ON HEAT

We covered this in the section on personal relationships. This is your body trying to make every last egg count.

Remember, you are still fertile at this point, and you can still get pregnant. It only takes one egg, even if it's your last. If the relationship is yet to be tested in any way, this may well be the very last thing you need to happen. For some women, however, this may be considered a miracle – they may have been thinking their time for children had passed.

CHAPTER 41
HOLDING OFF THE 'M' CONVERSATION

While timing is everything, I strongly suggest that a Menopause conversation is not for your first date, unless your symptoms are so extreme that you have to broach it. It could be the only way to preserve even a slim chance of a second date, as you need the opportunity to have the conversation on your terms and in an environment of your choosing.

As suggested, many partners may even by this age be unaware of much of what Menopause means or involves. Awareness does not guarantee comfort talking about it. And comfort talking about it does not guarantee acceptance or preparedness to understand that it's a phase of your life that will pass and not something that defines you. That means a Menopause conversation has to pass at least three tests – awareness, comfort and understanding. These are nondependent. That puts quite a burden on you and requires your calmest and most controlled self to navigate. Of course, it shouldn't be this way, and it shouldn't be your responsibility. Yet it is.

Even so, keep it light. They really don't need to know about the depths or the complexity of your Menopause at such an early stage.

If you are worried that you will get an intense hot flush, flooding or an attack of itching (formication), for example, run through how you might manage them.

For flushes and flooding, start with your clothes selection – see suggestions in the **Work** section. From there, pack a fan and/ or sanitary ware. The fan you might need to comment on, but they don't need to know about the towels in your handbag. At least not yet, anyway.

For the itching, wherever possible try not to start scratching and distract yourself. Some women use cooling moisturizer or an oatmeal colloidal while out, but declining oestrogen is at fault here. Seek assistance from your GP if needed.

When the two of you have grown a little closer, or if your symptoms are negatively impacting your behaviour, then you are likely to be at the point when you will need to have the 'M' conversation. Really, it shouldn't be such a big deal. You are both adults. Well, at least I hope your partner behaves like they are as you chose them because they were your equal.

CHAPTER 42
A SUCCESSFUL 'M' CONVERSATION WITH YOUR NEW PARTNER

You will have to have the 'M' conversation. Hiding it is not an option.

This is not the most romantic conversation you are going to have, nor is it one that you thought you would have to have, but have it you must. Especially if your symptoms are causing your moods to oscillate from loving to hateful, or teary to tantrum. If you are experiencing any of the disrupter symptoms in the intimacy section, it is likely you will need to discuss your Menopause before you get to that stage.

Your new partner is likely to be confused about the changes in you or your reticence to take the relationship into the bedroom. They will not understand the complexity of symptoms you are experiencing and how this affects you on a day-to-day basis. They really don't know the enormity of how you are feeling unless you tell them. They are not mind readers.

Choose a time when you know you won't be interrupted, whether that be by work, children, friends or their favourite TV programme. Next, try to ensure that the environment is calm. Seclusion is not always possible at home, so a private nook in a café or a walk in the park might be better. It's your call. Remember that you are about to be humble and vulnerable. You need to feel safe and wherever you choose needs to feel private.

Prepare what you are going to say. Use the work you did in Chapter 3 and Chapter 9, where you identified your symptoms and the interdependency work you did in **You Now**. Think in detail about what it is like for you, what happens and when. It is likely that you may need to reference the chronology of your core symptoms as well. This breadth of information will enable the other person to understand the complexity and depth of your experience.

We mentioned the three tests – awareness, comfort and understanding. Therefore, the first part of your conversation is awareness and education. You are supporting their learning so that they can help you through the ups and downs. Even if they have experienced a previous partner's Menopause or even their own, while it might be similar, it won't be the same.

GETTING OR ASKING FOR SUPPORT

Asking for support inside a new relationship is a much lighter touch than in an existing relationship. It is probable that you won't be living together or that they won't experience the worst of your symptoms.

Be reasonable and keep your gory details to a minimum. Always ask yourself if you would want to know the details. Conversely, asking for a bit of understanding when you are sweating it out is perfectly reasonable and to be encouraged.

KEEP IT SIMPLE

When thinking about what you are going to say, remember to be clear about the symptoms you are experiencing and their impact. Be factual. This should be relatively straightforward, as you will have established this already in **You Now**.

It's good to start by talking around what Menopause is in general, and then what it is for you specifically. If you are having extreme symptoms, it is likely that your new partner will be relieved that there is a normal explanation for the changes in you.

Next, be clear with yourself about what you want from this conversation and the help you want from your new partner. Make it easy. You are in a new relationship; don't overdramatize things. If your list is long and complex, most prospective partners may exit quickly. You will be painting a picture of high maintenance and unpredictability. What you are intending to describe are your symptoms and your strategies for controlling them. In reality, you are offering a picture of a woman in control. Even if at times you're not. Beyond that, you are asking for occasional assistance as and when appropriate, not an onsite nurse.

It is vital that you discuss Menopause as a phase. When a new relationship is forming, judgments are often made quickly and on limited evidence. That you are suffering hot flushes now does not mean that you are, for all time, sweaty. Therefore, a description of the symptoms over time can help, as this helps to portray the arrival and point to the eventual departure of Menopause. Think it through, be honourable and keep it simple.

MAINTAINING YOUR RELATIONSHIP

Now that you have declared that you are Menopausal and explained the symptoms that you are suffering from, work together to create some strategies to manage them.

As the relationship is new, most of the strategies fall to you. There is an opportunity, however, to create a two-way dialogue that can be helpful. In many respects, you have a chance to offer character-defining routes to getting help. Identifying and calling out behaviour that appears bonkers. Exploring amusing ways to help with memory loss. Ensuring fans are distributed in all the places you frequent. The journey needn't appear as a humourless path across eggshells.

Humility has a role to play, as does humour. The person you are being is not the person that you are, but much of the person you are can be exhibited when otherwise there may not have been an occasion. Show how amazing you are. If you apologize, do so lightly, because you can't help what's happening. See the 'M' conversation as an opportunity, not as a dark cloud about to unload.

My husband always joked that we were both suffering from Menopause, especially when he awoke in the night shivering with the quilt on the floor that I had cast off in despair. He claims to be an expert now. My youngest daughter would also state she was suffering from a hot flush when she was just hot. She always had a big smile on her face when she said it – she knew she was helping me through it. Support and help take many forms. Sometimes just a smile is enough.

MAINTAINING THE CONVERSATION

It is important to keep talking to your new partner, as they are unlikely to be aware of the nuances of your Menopausal experiences. Conversations of this type are not one-hit wonders. You shouldn't feel relief that it's over and done with. You will need to keep returning to it, not least because the severity of your symptoms will fluctuate as you move through your Menopause in parallel with the development and growth of your relationship. It is possible that you will gain some symptoms while losing others. If there are no outward signs that this is the case, there is no way your partner will be able to guess this.

We suggested that the second test was comfort. In many respects, Menopause offers an opportunity to create a relationship comfortable with all forms of difficult conversation, not just this one. You are defining your relationship by openness and sensitivity. Relationships characterized by withholding information of situations or feelings will be so across the board. Use Menopause to your advantage. Define yourself as open, empathetic, reasonable and wise.

Be prepared in all of this for some home truths regarding how difficult you can be. If this is the case, face it. Denying it shows disregard for your partner and the bond between you. You are also deceiving yourself and withholding an opportunity for you to take control. This is not a case of 'if I can't see it, it doesn't exist'. If you don't like that part of you and would rather ignore it, good luck. They don't go away so easily; in fact, they will continue to upset you both until you recognize them and take action. That moment of action passes the control from it to you.

New relationships are often full of excited plans for the future, travels, learning and a wide range of new experiences to bond the two of you together. Ensure that your five- and ten-year plans are honoured. Link them into your conversations and encourage your new partner to enter into your plans. Disregarding them at this early stage can be a point of contention later down the line. Your relationship will pass from 'me' to 'we'.

WHAT TO DO IF IT DETERIORATES

The third test is understanding, an unconditional preparedness to accept the situation and contribute with empathy and support. Without this, the fledgling relationship will deteriorate quickly.

If your new relationship does not survive this phase of your life, it is unfortunate, sad and disappointing. It is better, however, to learn this now than later down the line.

You are entering the second phase of your adult life and, most probably, so are they. You both will need to face adversity and challenging times. If the early bond between you is not strong enough to manage your Menopausal symptoms, then it is unlikely to be strong enough later on, to face other challenges that emerge later in life. It may transpire to have been a test worth taking to have found out.

The last place you want to be with a new relationship is arti-ficially clinging on. Unlike the relationships we have explored in this book, the vulnerability of new relationships usually means that deterioration signals the end. Allow yourself some time to feel the sadness of loss and then move on. It takes a little courage, and a commitment to yourself not to let it affect your confidence.

Be realistic as to why the relationship didn't work. Evaluate in a clear, cold manner. If for any reason Menopause or its effects were the cause, you can be entirely assured that it wasn't ever going to be the right one.

The silver lining in this situation is that you are progressing through your Menopause. You are continuing to reach the end of your transition and are coming ever closer to your post-Men-opausal self. You are growing in awareness and becoming more focused on where you wish to be. Your post-Menopausal self is formidable and will be so when seeking a new relationship too.

Each element of learning will enable you to more clearly identify the person you wish to be with. Who knows, you might be lucky enough for a sparkly unicorn to come clip-clopping up your drive. I was, but that's another story.

CHAPTER 43
SUMMARY

WHAT WE LEARNED

We learned that our perception of ourselves as intelligent and capable women is incredibly influential on our ability to find a suitable partner who inspires and excites us. As is our view of our body image: if we don't like what we see, how do we expect another to?

We learned the power of our own mind and how we can harness it to deliver to us the person we would like to be with.

We recognized that there are still users and wasters out there and that while disappointing, it is a necessary learning.

We discussed intimacy at this rapidly changing time and how our symptoms can cause complexity that we previously would not have had to manage.

This section would not have been complete without an 'M' conversation, yet with the subtleties needed for a new and developing relationship.

WHAT WE DID

We identified what we liked about ourselves – our mind, body and soul. We specified in detail the attributes of the person we would like to meet so that our superpowered brains can seek them out.

We confirmed the type of unwanted partners out there and how easy it is to be drawn in. Forewarned is forearmed.

HOW THIS HELPS

Taking control of our perceptions and our physical selves gives us the control that we lacked previously and empowers us to positively seek a partner. This gives us the sense of control often missing on the dating scene.

Facing new complexities brought on by your symptoms as an able and capable adult, while something you had hoped not to face, enables you to seek solutions and not suffer in silence.

Opening the conversation about your Menopause, while requiring delicate handling, is well within your capabilities, as is continuing the conversation.

We considered how Menopause may present itself as an opportunity to establish a bond in a new relationship.

Lastly, if this relationship is not to be, there is always a silver lining in that you are nearer to the end of your transition and your post-Menopausal self – and then you will be empowered by your reinvigorated second phase superpowers.

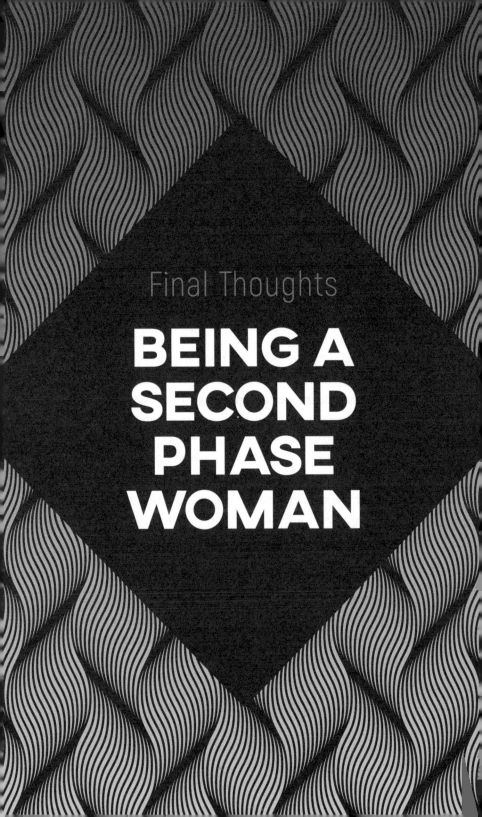

Final Thoughts

BEING A SECOND PHASE WOMAN

Your relationships – at work, in your personal life and those you have yet to craft – lie at the heart of your happiness, motivation and success. Maintaining and developing those relationships through the difficult time that Menopause presents is vital to your present and critical to your future. You have every possibility to grow them at this time – and every permission to ask for support from those around you.

Whatever your journey, remember that it is loaded with opportunity.

Throughout this book, you have been priming and honing your superpowers. It is quite possible that you didn't realize you had them or that you thought they had been in a race to the bottom, shackled to your declining oestrogen. You now know they are flexing and vibrating at a high frequency just beneath the surface.

We utilized your experience, skills, motivation, resilience, resources to create a desire for the second phase of your womanhood, to be optimistic and brimming with opportunities in whichever direction you choose.

Looking forward and planning your future directly connects you to ambitions and visions of what is to come. It frees your thinking and focuses on what is important to you and the future structure of your life. Once you have this, creating a pathway toward it becomes infinitely easier. The clarity you establish here creates the foundation for all other areas of your life.

Understanding what your symptoms are, how they show up, when they show up and your response to them when they do empowers you to take control. You can see their triggers, their beginnings or early warning signals, and create simple and effective processes to manage them and your response to them.

Teasing apart your symptoms instead of seeing them as one problematic mass gives you the opportunity to separate them and see any interconnectedness – that is, which symptoms influence or affect the others, sitting at the core of your experience. This enables you to either tackle the outer symptoms one by one or to go straight for the pack leader. You have the power to divide and conquer.

You are now in the driver's seat. Information is power, and you have what you need to manage this.

How you view yourself and communicate with yourself is critical. Appreciating who you are and who you will be – in mind, body and soul – will subliminally drive how others interact with you. Value yourself and others will too.

Conversation is at the core of managing your relationships successfully throughout your Menopause, whether that be at work or in your personal life. All your interactions will require you to think about what you ultimately want both in the micro and the macro – that is, from each conversation, building up to your five- and ten-year plan. All your relationships will require you to be the adult in the room, to be reasonable when asking for support, and to be honest with yourself and those around you. If you have been more difficult to manage than a bag of poisonous snakes, admit it. Focus, vulnerability and honesty are your allies and, when used correctly, they are most definitely superpowers in themselves.

Just as with your five- and ten-year plan, creating a joint plan with your partner will give you a focal point that will draw you through the difficult times and help to keep the bond between you strong.

If you are single, all attraction starts within. How you feel about yourself on the inside and out is incredibly powerful both in the negative and the positive. Valuing and cherishing yourself is a vital part of this process. This is not just in the physical sense, either. It is about recognizing who you are today and who you might be tomorrow, your lifestyle, your expectations and your needs. The power is in your clarity, your focus and your self-awareness.

Your hidden superpower in all of this is your brain. It is constantly seeking what you want. Whatever it is in life you have set your heart on, give your brain enough information, and it will seek it out continuously.

Being a second phase woman is extraordinary. You have the superpowers. Remember, this is not a pause in your life, and the post-Menopausal you will be unstoppable.

What is your story now – and what is it about to be?

FURTHER READING

The following is a non-exhaustive list of books you may find interesting and helpful.

MENOPAUSE

Abernethy, Kathy. *Menopause: The one-stop guide.* London: Profile Books Ltd, 2019.

Bluming, Avrum, and Carol Tavris. *Oestrogen Matters.* London: Piatkus, 2018.

Devlin, Ruth. *Men ... Let's Talk Menopause: What's going on and what you can do about it.* Tadley: Practical Inspiration Publishing, 2019.

Earle, Liz. *Healthy Menopause.* London: Boxtree, 1995.

Earle, Liz. *The Good Menopause Guide.* London: Orion Spring, 2018.

Foxcroft, Louise. *Hot Flushes, Cold Science: A history of the modern Menopause.* London: Granta, 2010.

Glenville, Marilyn. *Natural Solutions to Menopause: How to stay healthy before, during and beyond the Menopause.* London: Pan Macmillan, 2011.

Lewis, Jane. *Me & My Menopausal Vagina: Living with vaginal atrophy*. United Kingdom: PAL Books, 2018.

Mattern, Susan P. *The Slow Moon Climbs: The science, history, and meaning of Menopause*. New Jersey: Princeton University Press, 2019.

McLean, Andrea. *Confessions of a Menopausal Woman*. London: Corgi Books, 2019

Murray, Jenni. *Is It Me, or Is It Hot in Here?: A modern woman's guide to the Menopause*. London: Ebury Digital, 2012.

Newson, Louise. *Menopause: All you need to know in one concise manual*. Yeovil: Haynes, 2019.

Northrup, Christiane. *The Wisdom of Menopause: Creating physical and emotional health during the change*. New York: Bantam Books, 2012.

Ruddock, Jill Shaw. *The Second Half of Your Life*. London: Vermilion, 2015.

Wingert, Pat, Barbara Kantrowitz, and Bernadine Healy. *The Menopause Book: The Complete Guide: Hormones, hot flashes, health, moods, sleep, sex*. New York: Workman Publishing, 2018.

RELATIONSHIPS

Blackie, Sharon. *If Women Rose Rooted: A life-changing journey to authenticity and belonging.* Tewkesbury, Gloucestershire: September Publishing, 2019.

Chapman, Gary D. *The 5 Love Languages.* Chicago: Northfield Pub., 2015.

Gottman, John Mordechai, and Nan Silver. *The Seven Principles for Making Marriage Work.* London: Seven Dials, an imprint of Orion Publishing Group Ltd, 2018.

Payne, Martin. *Couple Counselling: A practical guide.* Los Angeles: Sage, 2010.

Perel, Esther. *Mating in Captivity.* London: Hodder & Stoughton, 2007.

SELF-ESTEEM, CONFIDENCE AND WELLBEING

Beard, Mary. *Women & Power: A manifesto.* London: Profile Books Ltd, 2018.

Dooley, Stacey. *On the Front Line with the Women Who Fight Back.* London: BBC Books, 2018.

Nadin, Gethin J. *A World of Good: Lessons from around the world in improving the employee experience.* CreateSpace Independent Publishing Platform, 2018.

Perez, Caroline Criado. *Invisible Women.*
London: Random House UK, 2019.

Wallace, Natasha. *The Conscious Effect: 50 lessons for better organizational wellbeing.* London: LID Business Media, 2019.

Walsh, Alyson. *Know Your Style: Mix it, match it, love it.*
London: Hardie Grant Books, 2017.

Walsh, Alyson, and Leo Greenfield. *Style Forever: How to look fabulous at every age.* Melbourne, Victoria: Hardie Grant Books, 2015.

COACHING AND CHANGE

Cooper, Lynne, and Mariette Castellino. *The Five-Minute Coach: Coaching others to high performance – in as little as five minutes.* Carmarthen: Crown House Publishing, 2012.

Lawley, James and Marian Way. *Insights in Space.*
Fareham: Clean Publishing, 2017.

Lawley, James, and Penny Tompkins. *Metaphors in Mind: Transformation through symbolic modelling.*
London: The Developing Company Press, 2013.

Sullivan, Wendy J., and Judy Rees. *Clean Language: Revealing metaphors and opening minds.* Bancyfelin: Crown House, 2009.

ENDNOTES

1   "Overview: Menopause." *NHS*. Accessed December 30, 2019. https://www.nhs.uk/conditions/menopause/.

2   Stöppler, Melissa Conrad. "Menopause Symptoms, Signs, Age, Herbal Remedies and Treatments." *eMedicineHealth*, September 6, 2019. https://www.emedicinehealth.com/menopause/article_em.htm.

3   "Overview: Menopause." *NHS*. Accessed December 30, 2019. https://www.nhs.uk/conditions/menopause/.

4   "Millions of Women Are Missing out on Hormone Replacement Therapy." *The Economist Newspaper*, December 12, 2019. Accessed December 30, 2019. https://www.economist.com/international/2019/12/12/millions-of-women-are-missing-out-on-hormone-replacement-therapy.

5   "British Menopause Society National Survey – the Results." *British Menopause Society*, March 2017. Accessed December 30, 2019. https://thebms.org.uk/wp-content/uploads/2016/04/BMS-NationalSurvey-MARCH2017.pdf.

6   "Suicides in the UK: 2017 registrations." *Office for National Statistics*. Accessed December 30, 2019. https://www.ons.gov.uk/peoplepopulationandcommunity/birthsdeathsandmarriages/deaths/bulletins/suicidesintheunitedkingdom/2017registrations#suicide-patterns-by-age.

7   "Suicides in the UK: 2018 registrations." *Office for National Statistics*. Accessed December 30, 2019. https://www.ons.gov.uk/peoplepopulationandcommunity/birthsdeathsandmarriages/deaths/bulletins/suicidesintheunitedkingdom/2018registrations.

8   Heller, J. *Catch 22*. London: Vintage, 1997.

9   "Find a BMS-Recognised Menopause Specialist." *British Menopause Society*, November 20, 2019. Accessed December 30, 2019. https://thebms.org.uk/find-a-menopause-specialist/.

10 Mattern, Susan P. *The Slow Moon Climbs: The science, history, and meaning of Menopause*. Princeton: Princeton University Press, 2019.

11   "A Woman's Relationship with the Menopause is Complicated."
British Menopause Society, October 2017. Accessed December 30, 2019.
https://thebms.org.uk/wp-content/uploads/2016/04/BMS-
Infographic-10-October2017-01C.pdf.

12   Endometriosis – where tissue similar to the lining of the uterus grows in
other places in the body. The condition usually ends after Menopause.

13   The Equal Pay Act 1970.

14   "Maternity (and Paternity) Leave and Pay." *Striking Women*.
Accessed December 30, 2019. https://www.striking-women.org/
module/workplace-issues-past-and-present/maternity-and-
paternity-leave-and-pay.

15   "Let's Talk Menopause: CIPD guidance." *CIPD*.
Accessed December 30, 2019. https://www.cipd.co.uk/
knowledge/culture/well-being/menopause.

16   "Female Employment Rate (Aged 16 to 64, Seasonally Adjusted)."
Office for National Statistics. Accessed December 30, 2019.
https://www.ons.gov.uk/employmentandlabourmarket/peopleinwork/
employmentandemployeetypes/timeseries/lf25/lms.

17   Newson, Dr Louise. "How Does the Menopause Affect Women at
Work." *My Menopause Doctor*. Accessed December 30, 2019.
https://www.menopausedoctor.co.uk/menopause/
how-does-menopause-affect-women-at-work.

18   "The Menopause: A workplace issue." *TUC*.
Accessed December 30, 2019. https://www.tuc.org.uk/sites/default/
files/Menopause survey report FINAL_0.pdf.

19   Hallett, Rachel, and Hutt, Rosamond. "10 Jobs That Didn't
Exist 10 Years Ago." *World Economic Forum*, June 7, 2016.
Accessed December 30, 2019. https://www.weforum.org/
agenda/2016/06/10-jobs-that-didn-t-exist-10-years-ago/.

20   "Business in the Community Age and Multigeneration Teams."
Business in the Community. Accessed December 30, 2019.
https://www.bitc.org.uk/age-and-multigeneration-teams/.

21   Gough, Owen. "Business Champion Calls for a Million More Older
People in Work by 2022." *Excellence in Diversity Awards*. Accessed
December 30, 2019. http://www.excellenceindiversity.co.uk/business-
champion-calls-for-a-million-more-older-people-in-work-by-2022.

22 "The Future of Work: Contingent workers and new employment." *Osborne Clarke*. Accessed December 30, 2019. https://www. osborneclarke.com/wp-content/uploads/2017/11/OC-The-Future-of-Work-Contingent-workers-8pp-A4-36099747-SOFT.pdf.

23 "Understanding the Risks of Breast Cancer." *British Menopause Society*, November 2015. Accessed December 30, 2019. https://thebms.org.uk/wp-content/uploads/2016/04/WHC-UnderstandingRisksofBreastCancer-MARCH2017.pdf.

24 "What People Recovering From Alcoholism Need To Know About Osteoporosis." *U.S. Department of Health and Human Services*. Accessed December 30, 2019. https://www.bones.nih.gov/health-info/bone/osteoporosis/conditions-behaviors/alcoholism#b.

25 "10 Leading Causes of Death in Females." *World Health Organization*, December 13, 2010. Accessed December 30, 2019. https://www.who.int/gho/women_and_health/mortality/situation_trends_causes_death/en/.

26 Merchant vs BT plc (2012) and Davis vs Scottish Courts & Tribunal Service (2017).

27 Unpublished diagram by Neil Usher. Icons from the Noun Project.

28 "Health and Wellbeing at Work." *CIPD*. Accessed December 30, 2019. https://www.cipd.co.uk/knowledge/culture/well-being/health-well-being-work.

29 The quality and timeliness of your outputs are valued more highly than your physical presence in the workplace.

30 Peter, Laurence J., and Raymond Hull. *The Peter Principle*. London: Souvenir Press, 1969.

31 Lunden, Ingrid. "HappyOrNot Raises $25M for Its Customer Satisfaction Terminals for Stores and Other Locations." *TechCrunch*, September 19, 2019. https://techcrunch.com/2019/09/19/happyornot-raises-25m-for-its-customer-satisfaction-terminals-for-stores-and-other-locations/.

32 Duhigg, Charles. "What Google Learned From Its Quest to Build the Perfect Team." *The New York Times*. February 25, 2016. https://www.nytimes.com/2016/02/28/magazine/what-google-learned-from-its-quest-to-build-the-perfect-team.html.

33 Brown, Brené. *Daring Greatly: How the courage to be vulnerable transforms the way we live, love, parent and lead*. Harmondsworth: Penguin Publishing Group, 2012.

34 In conversation with Kathy Abernethy, author of *Menopause: The one-stop guide*. London: Profile Books Ltd, 2019.

35 Professor Anne MacGregor in a talk, "Hormones and Headache" at the British Menopause Society 29th Annual Scientific Conference. Kenilworth, July 4, 2019.

36 "Magnesium – How It Affects Your Sleep." *The Sleep Doctor*, November 27, 2019. Accessed December 30, 2019. https://thesleepdoctor.com/2017/11/20/magnesium-effects-sleep/.

37 "The Menopause: A workplace issue" *TUC*. Accessed December 30, 2019. https://www.tuc.org.uk/sites/default/files/ Menopause survey report FINAL_0.pdf.

38 This quote has been attributed to Sun Tzu, Niccolò Machiavelli, Shakespeare and even the fictional Michael Corleone in the film *The Godfather Part II* (1974) by Mario Puzo and Francis Ford Coppola.

39 Matrimony and Family proceedings Act 1984.

40 Chang, Ha-Joon. *23 Things They Don't Tell You about Capitalism*. New York: Bloomsbury Press, 2010.

41 Barr, Sabrina. "Women Still Do the Majority of Household Chores, Study Finds." *Independent Digital News and Media*, July 26, 2019. https://www.independent.co.uk/ life-style/women-men-household-chores-domestic-house-gender-norms-a9021586.html.

42 Northrup, Christine. *The Wisdom of Menopause: Creating physical and emotional health and healing during the change*. New York: Bantam Books, 2012.

43 "Find a BMS-Recognised Menopause Specialist." *British Menopause Society*, November 20, 2019. https://thebms.org.uk/find-a-menopause-specialist/.

44 "Vaginal Dryness." Women's Health Concern, August 7, 2018. https://www.womens-health-concern.org/help-and-advice/ factsheets/vaginal-dryness/.

45 Aesop, and Thomas James. *Aesop's Fables: A new version, chiefly from orginal sources.* New York: Leavitt & Allen, 1861.

46 Chapman, Gary D. *The 5 Love Languages.* Chicago: Northfield Pub., 2015.

47 "Dataset: Divorces in England and Wales." *Office for National Statistics.* Accessed December 30, 2019. https://www.ons.gov.uk/peoplepopulationandcommunity/birthsdeathsandmarriages/divorce/datasets/divorcesinenglandandwales.

48 "Ruth Westheimer Interview." *The Guardian*, May 12, 2019. Accessed December 30, 2019. https://www.theguardian.com/global/2019/may/12/still-talking-about-sex-dr-ruth-westheimer-interview.

49 Kerr, Judith. *The Tiger Who Came to Tea.* Somerville, MA: Candlewick Press, 2019.

50 Levine, Laura E., and Joyce Munsch. *Child Development: An active learning approach.* Thousand Oaks, California: Sage, 2011.

51 A practice by which people put their car keys in bowl with the intention of 'drawing' a partner at random with whom to spend the night.

52 Comfort, Alex and Quilliam, Susan. *The Joy of Sex.* New York: Harmony Books, 2015.

53 *Fatal Attraction*, 1987.

54 "Divorces in England and Wales: 2017." *Office for National Statistics.* Accessed December 30, 2019. https://www.ons.gov.uk/peoplepopulationandcommunity/birthsdeathsandmarriages/divorce/bulletins/divorcesinenglandandwales/2017.

55 British family game show, broadcast by the BBC.

56 "Values in Action." *Changing Minds.* Accessed December 30, 2019. http://changingminds.org/explanations/values/via.htm.

57 Greenemeier, Larry. "Analyzing What Robots Tell Us About Human Nature: A Q&A with Will Wright." *Scientific American*, March 23, 2009. https://www.scientificamerican.com/article/will-wright-qa/.